To

Diane

Thank you

So very much

for being such

a...

[signature]

3/9/2_

The Journey to Chatham

Why Emmett Till's Murder
Changed America,
a personal story

by

Arthur L. Miller

authorHOUSE™

1663 LIBERTY DRIVE, SUITE 200
BLOOMINGTON, INDIANA 47403
(800) 839-8640
WWW.AUTHORHOUSE.COM

First published by AuthorHouse 08/26/05

ISBN: 1-4208-7544-2 (sc)
ISBN: 1-4208-7545-0 (dj)

Library of Congress Control Number: 2005906968

Printed in the United States of America
Bloomington, Indiana

This book is printed on acid-free paper.

Cover by Guy Blais

Preface

Jeffrey O. Green Ogbar PhD.

Coming of age stories are as varied and rich as the people who have them to tell. They often provide insight, nostalgic humor, and "those-were-the-days," tropes. They resonate with us because we can identify with the awkward innocence of youthful awakening. For a generation of African Americans the tragic story of Emmett Till was an unwelcome awakening and introduction to America's terrible practice of inhumanity to its own. While this particular story revolves around a tragedy that would become a major instigator of the civil rights movement, it is much more than the story of the Till murder. It is a tale that is generally universal: childhood exploration, family, love, hurt, crushes and bullies.

This story is intimately told and resonates with me for several reasons. It is a story of my family. My father, Jeffrey, Sr., and his cousin Pete Miller, joined Emmett Till in Till's last classroom photo in 1954. My father appears on the same row as Till, separated by three classmates. My aunts, uncles and cousins (from both sides of the family) attended school with Till and recount the horror they experienced at his murder. As a history professor, I discuss the impact of the Till case on the civil rights movement. While my students are often horrified by the story, the case helps contextualize the world of race in

America. It helps them understand the fervor and zeal of black and white civil rights activists who sacrificed so much for freedom. But even as I teach the subject, I find myself learning more about it constantly. I recently learned that my maternal grandmother and aunt attended the Till funeral. With this book I learned that my paternal great aunt Helen was also one of over ten thousand who viewed Till's open casket. The Till tragedy was not just in Chicago, though; it was national in scope. This was particularly clear when the Eisenhower administration chose not to charge the Till defendants with violations of Till's civil rights after the acquitted men admitted to the murder in a national magazine.

Beyond the larger story of Till, this story helps add insight and perspective to a rich cultural landscape of African Americans in one of the most storied black communities in the country. Chicago had become, by the late-1950s, the most residentially segregated city in the United States. Its Black Belt was home to the country's largest contiguous black community and a vibrant black world that functioned as a veritable city of its own. Forced into a huge section of the city's South Side, the Black Belt was home to over a half a million African Americans, including professionals, blue collar workers and the poor, often living in the same neighborhoods. Many people, born and raised in this area had no meaningful contact with whites: no whites over for dinner, at churches, in fraternities, sororities, or social clubs. Similarly, the whites in Chicago (or any other city) could not recount any black dinner guest or social intimate. Despite the stark degree of social distance in America, sometimes interactions between the groups forced white and black Americans to confront the ugly reality of racial oppression for the monster it is.

America, in the 1950s, was much more than idyllic nuclear families experiencing middle class affluence in the suburbs. It was more than the emergence of teen culture and its sonic background, rock and roll. It was broader than the shamefully innocuous terms "segregation" or Jim Crow, which are used to describe the racial landscape of the era. Millions of American citizens could not vote, get quality jobs, education, housing or equal protection simply because they were not white. They were victims of a brutal system of racial subjugation that could endorse the murder of children such as Emmett Till, for infractions against white supremacy.

Despite these loathsome circumstances however, black people managed to create full lives for themselves. Arthur Miller demonstrates here, that there were spaces in which people, in the midst of so much hate, continued to cultivate love, respect and a celebration of life. It was not a perfect world without problems. It was a varied world of experiences that formed the diverse tapestry of young people coming of age and the families that did their best to protect, guide, love, and nurture them. Vividly told with wonderful historical vignettes that appear organic and never forced, this memoir reaches out to all and resonates with universality. It extends beyond the Miller family to families untold in numbers.

Contents

Acknowledgements

The first of course is to God, for I know to whom I belong and to whom I give all praise and honor. I acknowledge the glory of the one who saved me.

I am eternally grateful to so many people who have helped in this task. It has been a glorious pursuit, as the ghosts in my memory played hide and seek with me.

Countless numbers have supported this journey with countless moments of encouragement and love. To them I am so thankful.

Guy Blais, your desire for peace in the world is admirable and achievable. I appreciate your honesty, your frankness, your patriotism, and, most of all, your editing skills.

Nancy Hooper, your work is outstanding, thank you.

Tom McMillan, a teacher at Owen D. Young School, you gave me an insight for transitions for this story that were helpful and useful.

David Holdt, teacher and dear friend, your patience and willingness to read, and reread, and reread were important to the completion of this effort. I am so grateful to you and the rest of the Watkinson family.

The teachers, staff, and students at Fisher Elementary School in Mohawk, New York, it is there that I began telling the story. I appreciate your dedication and commitment to your community, especially Ms. Janicki, Ms. Noonan, Ms. Williams, Ms. Aney, and Ms. Laporte. The teachers and students at Herkimer High School, especially Scott Clarke, who first invited me, thank you. The teachers and students at Cherry Valley-Springfield School, your attention and commitment to our society are admirable. Thanks, Keith Blankley and Margaret Bouck, for inviting me. To the students and teachers at Edmeston Central School, particularly Mrs. Christiansen, her husband Andy, and their daughter Emily, thank you for listening and caring.

Special friends: Fr. James Ibekwe, Sister Pat Chappell, Sister Kendra Bottoms and Mrs. Bottoms, Frs. Anthony Bozeman and Richard Russell, I thank you for your honesty and commitment to those you serve.

My fellow Deacons, particularly the class of 2004: six long years, what a ride.

Dennis and Linda Ferguson, thank you for your kindnesses and love.

St. Justin's family: The church choir, you are the heart and soul of your church. Keep the faith, Hazel, Debbie Boyd, Mrs. Green, Kay Taylor-Brooks, Myles Hubbard.

St. Michael's Church family: Father Al Janiceke, Father Dave McDonald, Father Arlin Jean-Louis, Deacon Tom Breen, Sister Betty Secord, Joey and Jackie Arango and family, Donna Shears and family, Harry and Cheryl Lawrence, Marian Glassee, Jonette Franklin, Vivian Cicero, the Christie family, Sharon Barnes, Lew Brown, Bob Brown, Kenneth McBride, Ellsworth Grant, Libby Gray, Alex and Kara Mikulich and family, Brian and Arlene Harris and family, Vernette and Rich Soutar and their daughters, Jose Cotto, Yvonne Colon, Leticia Hilliman, Brenda Colon and son, and Victor Cruse. Your advice and support helped fill the gaps in my soul.

The choir at St. Michael's, you have made my worship of God more beautiful because of your wonderful voices. Thank you.

The Spanish community, *me hermanos y hermanas in Cristo, gracias.* The best cup of café I have ever had was at *La Paloma Sabanera* in Hartford, Ct. *Gracias.*

Brother Knights of Peter Claver and the Ladies Auxiliary, your prayerful support has gotten me through the valleys.

UCONN medical students Damian, Cynthia, Laura, Akim, what a wonderful example you are. Thank you for the inspiration.

The Monday evening golf league at Keney Park, you gave me time to laugh, play and to be with my brothers. Thanks, Evans Jacobs, for critically reading my efforts.

Stephen Christmas, Freddy Moore, the Cage clan, especially Frances, thank you for the 50s.

Good friends, Ann Ford, the Taylors, Judy Struthers, thank you for your friendship and love. Harold and Margaret Stoffolano, thanks for trusting me.

C. Steven Robinson, you are a part of the story of my life. Thanks for being a part of my construction. Brenda thanks for keeping him humble.

Jimmy Wang, my journey was made easier because of our friendship. Thank you.

Alicia Lipe, the girl who scared me as much as Frances.

Lucia Bell, the girl who scared me after Alicia.

My daughters-in-law, Damaris and Kirsten, you have loved my sons. Thank you for being a part of us.

My family: Aunt Charlotte, Uncle Herman, Uncle Ronnie, and cousin Hank, you are the last of your generation to travel the difficult road that had to be walked. Thank you for your undying courage. For Uncle Johnny, Aunt Edith, and Carolyn, I thank you for your gifts to this family and to me.

Mickey, thanks for the fishing trips to Washington Park and for looking out for me when I didn't know how.

Billy, you are the key to so much good. Thank you for believing in me.

Jeff Sr., you were a piece of work. Thank you for your son. You would be so proud.

Jeff Jr., thank you for your spirit. Your father lives through you.

Little Helen, I am so proud of you. You have made it through hell. I believe that yours is the story that should be told. You have my complete respect and admiration.

Reggie, Donald, Kenny, and Karen, thank you for being so cool.

Leticia, Terry, and Gregory Smith, I remember so many wonderful times with you. Hold dear to the good of your present and your past.

Jay Robinson and family, continue holding on to all the truths of your origin, they are wonderful.

My mother-in-law, Mrs. Fletcher Mae Gilliam-Hopson-Bazemore, thank you for loving me and believing in me. Lenwood, thank you for making her happy at sunset.

James Hopson, you were the strongest man I have ever known. I pray that you approve.

Debbie and Rufus, thank you for being a wonderful example of beauty and strength.

Penny and Judy, I have known you for so long. Thank you for your many kindnesses.

William, you and Andi continue our story. Know it and share it.

My nephews and nieces, Kathi, Bobby, David, Jonathan, Deana, Vernon, Matthew, Dannon, and Ryanne, this story is also for you.

Jon, your efforts inspired mine. Thank you.

My brothers and sisters, Carol, Pete, Marty and Andi, you have been partners, friends, and protectors in this journey. My thanks to you are imbedded in the pages of this book.

To my children, Nikki, Adam, Jason and Sam, it is for you and your children that I began this story. Nikki, welcome back. Adam, you read and reread more than anyone, you challenged and questioned what I did not explain well. I appreciate the effort and help. Much of what I wrote is attributable to you. You have the gift of patience and love. Thank you. Jason, thank you for so many years of joy. You were my sanity for longer than you know. Sam, you have been the gift of joy and love for your mom and me. We are so proud of you. FOREVER.

To my grandchildren, Kobie, Akeeva, Desiree, Briana, and you who have yet to be born, read to know your past. It is the foundation for your future.

Dad, you were a man who loved and protected us. I never felt afraid. Thank you.

Mom, there can never be a moment in my life that you do not affect. I cherish my remembrances of you. Your patience with me was worthy of sainthood.

Sandy, my beloved wife, I have searched my memory for words of love that I have not yet told you and found there are none, for I have told you countless times and numberless ways how much I do love you. Were it possible, I would take all the languages of the world and combine them to create new expressions that would encompass the breadth, and width, and depth, of my love for you. Even if that were possible, those new words would tumble upon themselves, knowing it was futile, for no words can reveal the fullness of my love. I can only be in love with you, telling you is too small.

Chapter one

In the Beginning

"Oh, God!!!! NOOO!! MA! MA! Oh, please, NOOO!"

Somewhere in the universality of time, the pain in my brother's scream still exists. It hangs there, naked, coldly carrying the hurts, injustices, crimes, and horrific ugliness that scarred the soul of America. For our family, on our streets, and in our country, time separated itself into two periods, before Emmett and after Emmett. We may not have known it then, but with the barbaric murder of Emmett Till, the world began to see what America was and what it was not.

Chicago during the summer of 1955 was much like most northern U.S. cities. An odd sort of peace existed between blacks and whites. Most black people understood what they were allowed to do and what they were not. They were willing to live with that reality because they believed as long as they were freer than the families they had left down South, the racism they had to face up North wasn't that bad. There was a strange feeling of insulation from the overt racial barbarism and brutality that existed in the South. But that changed violently and completely with Emmett's death. Barbarism came home to stay, wrapped in the mutilated, broken body of a 14-year-old little boy.

The day we found out Emmett had been murdered my family was away on vacation, at our farm in Michigan. I had just awakened to the sound of an old rooster's call when I heard my brother Pete's scream pierce what had been an otherwise beautiful morning. My mother quickly gathered my brothers and me into the little breezeway of the farmhouse as the sun slowly slid behind a wandering cloud, which caused the small room to lose its warmth. We boys sat on the sun-faded couch that faced a large picture window. On that old couch we often watched wild birds swoop over the abandoned meadow that stretched out from the house. At the edge of the meadow stood an old barn that leaned heavily to one side, like a drunken sailor who had seen too many storms.

Mom stood near my two brothers and me, motionless, brooding, arms wrapped around her. The newspaper she had taken from my brother lay crumbled at her feet. She slowly caressed her temple and massaged it. She needed to explain to us what had happened to Emmett.

"Ahhhmm, boys."

At that moment the phone rang. My father walked to the phone that was in the room near the breezeway and answered it. It was my 17-year-old sister Carol, who was back in Chicago. I could hear Dad talking to her on the phone. She had heard about Emmett's death. My dad, usually not the gentlest of people, was uncharacteristically kind and caring toward my sister. He was trying to calm her, using soothing words I had never heard come from him.

"Carol, I know it is hard for you because your mom and I aren't there. You'll be OK. Now, we'll be home in a few days…. Yes. I know I know, honey. You'll be all right. Yes, I'll have your mom call you back. Yes, he's all right. She's talking to him now… Yes, to all your brothers now… Yes, honey, all three. OK, I'll tell them."

Dad murmured a few more words, hung up, and walked into the little breezeway where my brothers and I sat. Mom looked at the three of us huddled together on the couch. She started to say something, caught herself, and then started again.

"Boys, something horrible lives in this country. It's called racism and prejudice. It's time…it is…time for you to understand…what it means…to be a Negro in America."

Mom's voice cracked; this was clearly painful for her. She bent down and looked at us, gently touching the top of Pete's head. He was curled in a tight ball whimpering and hiccuping every few seconds. Instead of looking at my mom's eyes, I watched as her hand gently rubbed Pete's forehead. I could barely recognize him. The features of this 12-year-old boy suddenly appeared to be ancient. Whatever caused my older brother to scream like that, to look like that, must have been horrible.

I looked at Marty, my younger brother, who was sitting next to me, his big brown eyes reflecting the fear a seven year old has for the unknown. He was silent.

"Your friend Emmett, remember the boy in Pete's class? I think you guys had a nickname for him—Bobo or Bo? Well, he was killed!" Mom was abrupt.

She was a tall, elegant woman with light brown features. Her skin was smooth, unwrinkled by time and worry. She had freckles, but not too many, that created an interesting pattern on her face. I had often tried to draw pictures by connecting the freckles on her face. She had a gentle soul and had always been patient with me, but now she didn't look pretty, or gentle. She looked angry, like an ancient being that sensed a predator stalking her brood. I didn't understand what was going on, but it was life changing, severe in its importance.

With every mention of Emmett's name, Pete shuddered, hiccupping over and over. Mom sat down next to Pete and held him. A tear squeezed from one of her eyes and slowly found its way down her freckled cheek. She wiped it away with the tips of her fingers.

We had seen her cry before, usually when she watched a sad movie. But, every so often, we would catch her crying softly while watching us play. It was something she did that we didn't quite understand, because while she cried, she wore a slight smile under her tears. This was not that kind of crying.

"Mom.... Mom. Do you mean that kid that sat next to Pete in school? You mean Bo? He died? How? When? You can't die when you're a kid! Only old people like grandparents die!"

As a 10 year old, I couldn't figure out how a child could die. My great-grandmother, my dad's grandmother, had died. She died because she was old, and that made sense. Hers had been my only experience with death. How could a kid die? Kids were young; they didn't know what they were going to be yet. How can someone who hadn't grown up to be something or do something die? How can you die when you really hadn't gotten to be who you were going to be? This whole thing didn't make any sense, yet.

When Emmett was lynched, we were on the farm my parents and Uncle Herman had bought. It was about 150 miles from Chicago in Three Rivers, Michigan. We went there often, and to us, it was a wonderland. The farm was on 80 acres. It had an old whitewashed farmhouse with four small bedrooms, a bathroom upstairs and one downstairs, a dining room, and a living room. It had a breezeway that had an old couch where we sat and watched summer storms and a huge kitchen. Linoleum, yellowed by time and use, covered the kitchen's wood-planked floor.

A pump in the sink had to be hand-pumped five or six times before cold, clear-spring water burst from the spout. I was too small to reach the iron handle and not strong enough to budge it when I stood on a chair.

The farm was bought in 1949 with money Uncle Herman had saved while in the Army, which was combined with money my parents had put away. It was a safe place for my uncle and his white German war bride.

We loved it and spent hours and hours hiking along paths we had made that wove haphazardly through the wild wheat fields. The sweet smell was permanent. At night, we listened to evening noises that drifted in through open bedroom windows as soft summer breezes sent us into deep slumber. Evening stars pocked the black night like 4th of July sparklers.

A stand of woods 300 yards behind the house held the secrets of our hunting games and searches for garter snakes. We went there often to feel the cool, benevolent silence. We believed that January never arrived, snow never fell, and cold lifeless winters never chilled our summer home. It was a magical place where every month was July and every day was Saturday.

But now the world had changed and everything was different. A frigid, unnatural evil had entered our lives. A friend, a neighborhood kid, was dead. I was soon to find out how.

Mom sighed, "You know that Emmett went down to Mississippi to visit his family this summer. Well, it seems that he got into some kind of trouble with some white people."

"Mom, what kinda trouble? Did he tease somebody?" Marty had found his voice.

"No, baby, not like that," she responded.

She was exhausted; this wasn't going to be easy. How do you teach children about hate? Should kids be protected from learning about hate, or should they be protected by learning about hate? It is a hard question that forces even more difficult answers, life-altering answers.

What she told us that last day of August was the height and depth and width of human profanity. Emmett had been murdered by a hatred that was ignored by a society that professed fellowship. In a country that fought for freedom from tyranny overseas, an inhumane horror thrived at home. Emmett's murder was profane in its occurrence and heinous for being tolerated.

Mom showed us the local newspaper Pete had been reading. The headlines read, "Chicago Teen Murdered in Mississippi." The paper reported the story of Emmett's death. In gruesome detail the article recounted how he was found and the condition of his body. For us there was no more innocence. A part of us died that day along with Emmett, a very innocent part. All of us were changed on that warm August day, changed because a hatred we could not fathom oozed up from the bottom of a Mississippi river.

While Mom comforted us, I watched as Dad stared out the front window at the old walnut tree in the front yard. From one of the lower branches dangled an old tire that we used as a makeshift swing. It dangled from a rope we had tied to one of the lower branches. I could see the tire spin as it reacted to a breeze that had just kicked up.

My dad was not big; he never weighed more than 155 pounds. At 5'9" he was wiry, muscular. He was a singularly handsome man who wore his jet-black, wavy-hair straight back over his head. In the back of his neck, in what was referred to as the "kitchen," a mass of black curls congregated. He wore his white blood on his face and was as close to an Errol Flynn look-alike as one could get. Yet he was unmistakably a black man. His good looks were a curse and a blessing. As a milkman he had developed strong arms and hands from carrying cases of milk to his customers. But at this moment he didn't look strong. He looked small, frail, as if he had shrunken into himself. I couldn't imagine his thoughts.

Above his shoulders, I could see the fields through the window. The tire spun lazily at the end of the rope. The wind picked up a few newly fallen leaves that did little dances in a small barren patch in the front yard. The sky reflected the mood; it had turned bleak. Off, far off, there was a deep, long groan. Thunder. A storm was coming.

Pete still sniffed back tears, while Marty squeezed onto Mom's lap, frightened by the fear in the air, his seven-year-old mind shaken by the strangeness that had come over his family.

The newspaper story detailed the condition of Emmett's body when he was found. It was bloated from being in the river for three days. He had gunshot holes in his head. The results of a severe beating were still evident, despite the deterioration of his body from the water. Barbed wire had been tied around his neck and attached to a 70-pound cotton gin, which was done to weigh his body down and keep it from rising up from the bottom of the Tallahatchie River. His fingers and other appendages were crushed. He had been tortured. His face was so battered that he was unrecognizable. The only clue of who he was, was the signet ring he wore on his finger. It had belonged to Emmett's father, who was killed during World War II.

I wondered what was going on back home in Chicago. What would happen when we got back? I wondered whether the city would be changed because a kid died. Would everyone where we lived, 64th and Vernon Avenue on the south side, be changed? Would the kids I went to school with change?

A kid died. A kid I knew died.

I remembered Emmett. His face was round, full, with hazel eyes like my brother Pete. Everyone who knew him called him "Bo." He stuttered a little bit. When he got excited, he had to whistle to get his voice going.

We all went to McCosh elementary on 65th and Champlain Avenue, about five blocks from our home. Every day kids would walk to and from school. My brothers and I along with our cousins, who lived in the same apartment building, would make the daily journey together. Boys would have their Duncan Yoyo's trying to do tricks all the way to school. Girls had their jump ropes. You could see an occasional double-dutch routine on the way.

"2-4-6-8-10-12-14-16-18-22-32-42-52-62-72-82-92-100" the rhythmic chants of little girls' rope jumping songs filled the air. "22-32-42 and don't forget those red hot beans."

Then the jump rope would accelerate, dancing legs pumping, hands a blur as the girls turned their ropes, pigtails flying and heads bobbing with the rhythm of the song. The rope turning so fast it was almost invisible. Little girl shoes smacking the pavement.

Wap-wap-wap-wap.

The rope hitting the pavement on each turn. Fap-fap-fap-fap.

Wap-fap-wap-fap-wap-fap.

Laughter, kids skipping, running, walking together. It was a symphony—the music of the young.

A long, steady stream of children swept along with classmates and friends, filling the neighborhood streets, making their way to school through alleys and backyards, through empty lots, like ants invading a virgin forest. Doorways emitted their progeny as empty lots lost the sound of baseball, hopscotch, and tag, a hodgepodge of children, small, large, tall, short, fat, skinny. Laughter echoed off the walls of the buildings, a concrete canyon, as the river of children made their daily walk.

Emmett was one of many kids who went to McCosh Elementary School. My brothers and I all walked to school together. Occasionally, Emmett walked with us. Pete, Emmett, and our cousin Jeffrey were in Mrs. Campbell's class. Pete was small and very smart. In fact, he had skipped fourth grade and had gone straight to fifth grade after third.

Sometimes he was the target for the bigger boys' teasing. They bullied him not for being smart; on the contrary, most admired him for that. It was because he was small and quiet and they were bigger. Generally, the teasing was good-natured. Pete didn't like it though.

I remembered Emmett primarily because of an incident that had happened the previous summer. He was quieter back then and had difficulty speaking. Most everyone liked Emmett. It was hard not to, he was a very funny kid.

In Chicago, our home was a one-bedroom apartment. My parents, my sister, my two brothers, and I lived on the top floor of a three-story apartment building. It was a warm and wonderful place to grow up. On the second floor of our building were my mom's sister, Aunt Ramona, her husband, Uncle Jimmy, and their three sons, Mickey, Jeffrey, and Billy. We were all close to the same age, so we had playmates close by. In bad weather we could still see each other because we were in the same building.

The neighborhood was a mixture of every kind of individual and family. Our block had three-story apartment buildings, about 10 of them. Each building had six apartments. In addition to the three-story apartment buildings, the block also had several two-story buildings with four apartments. Surprisingly, the neighborhood also had 10 to 12 individual homes.

On our side of the street alone, nearly 80 families lived, doctors and dentists, nurses, schoolteachers, the very well-educated folks as well as the near illiterate. There were blue-collar workers like my dad, a milkman. My mom was a secretary. Even though she had been to college, during the mid-20th century, it was nearly impossible for a black woman to find white-collar work.

All of us living in the community looked out for one another. Any problem was a community problem. All this would change with the effects of Emmett's death. The events that followed altered forever the landscape of America. Little did the hate-filled men who killed Emmett Till that horrible night know that they were unleashing the most incredible reform to ever shake the foundation of America, the most powerful country in the world.

Following the Civil War, for black folk in the South as well as the North, things didn't change all that much. It was the civil rights movement that black people fought that changed America for us. The first martyr, the catalyst for that incredible movement, rose out of the Talahatchee River near Money, Mississippi, August 31, 1955.

The last day of our vacation was spent in virtual silence. My mother had explained that many white people hated black people, especially in the South. Hated us because they felt we were inferior, or not as smart, or as good as white people.

"But, Mom, does Aunt Chris, or did Bubby hate us, too? Or what about Little Helen?"

Marty wondered about some of the white people in our family. Chris was our Uncle Herman's wife, a German war bride my uncle had married right after World War II; little Helen was their daughter. She was called "Little" Helen because she was named after my mom, Helen. (My mom, however, made it perfectly clear that she was not, and never would be called, "Big" Helen.) Little Helen wasn't white; but with very straight blond hair and blue eyes, it was impossible to see her mixed heritage. Bubby, our great-grandmother, was born in Czechoslovakia and had spoken with a very-heavy Slavic accent. She had died the previous summer.

"No, honey, not all of them. There are certainly many good white people, just as there are many good Negroes. However, a long time ago, Africans were brought to this country. They were brought to this country as slaves."

"Kids, too?"

Marty was anxious to understand.

"Yes, kids, too," Mom replied sadly.

"But, Mom, why bring kids here? Don't slaves have to work real hard and do crappy stuff? Kids can't do that, cause they didn't go to school to learn nothin' to do."

Marty's seven-year-old mind wasn't handling this talk well.

Mom hesitated, trying to figure out a way to arm her precious children to teach them to be careful, but not to frighten them. Yet, to frighten them, frighten them enough to save them.

"Boys, I want you to listen to me. I will answer any questions you have. But for now, just listen."

We had never seen Mom like this.

"Slavery here in America began very early. You know about Columbus and his discovering America. Well, the truth is, there were people here already. And you can't discover something that someone has already discovered. But for some white people, the Indians that were already here didn't matter. They were thought to be savages or uncivilized. So, soon after that the white people who had come here from Europe tried to make the Indians do a lot of the very difficult work. But the Indians would run away. So the white people went to Africa and kidnapped millions of the people there, then brought them thousands of miles over the ocean and made them do the really hard work here as slaves. They couldn't run away, because their homes were too far away."

My brothers and I were stunned. This was new information. I had never read about any of this or learned about any of this at school.

"To feel OK, or to justify their terrible crime against the people of Africa, white people had to believe the African people were not quite human. That way the white people wouldn't feel bad about what they had done. Even today, many white people and even some Negroes feel that all of this is true. They believe that Negroes are not as good as white people. It is something you will always have to fight against. You are not bad, or dumb, or anything like that. Always believe that you are good, and smart, and wonderful little boys. You will also be very good and strong men when you grow up. This is very important to remember. No matter what people try to tell you. Always, always remember that you are smart and good. You must always show people that, no matter what. Remember."

Columbus didn't discover America? In a very simple way, Mom had encapsulated a basic human truth. Whenever one race attempts to dehumanize another, believing them to be uncivilized savages, those who do the dehumanizing are uncivilized in their savagery. The long struggle for human dignity is what all black Americans would face and wrestle with for all of their lives.

Pete, Marty, and 'Little' Helen on the farm,
Three Rivers, Michigan circa 1950

Chapter two

The Neighborhood

We returned to Chicago the day after learning of Emmett's death; my parents decided we could no longer stay on vacation. The drive home took three hours, but it seemed much longer. Things were different. I'm not sure whether it was us, or the neighborhood, or the air— maybe it was all of it—but things were different. The closer we got to Chicago, the more you could feel it.

We came back to the home we loved and cherished, that had always been safe and familiar. I knew our apartment and the neighborhood as well as I knew the inside of my own mouth. It was a part of who I was, who my family was, where everything fit into place.

In 1941 my parents moved with Carol from the West Side of Chicago to the apartment on the South Side. Carol was three years old at the time, and because my parents were planning to have more children, they needed a larger place. The one-room efficiency where they had been living was much too small, and they were tired of sharing the bathroom and kitchen with other families in the boarding house. For many young families in Chicago and other large cities during the 1930s this was common.

The spacious one-bedroom apartment they found was perfect; it was in a building that stood on a beautiful street shaded by century-old elm trees. Each apartment had its own bathroom and kitchen that meant the resident would have privacy and space. The private kitchen and bathroom was an unfamiliar yet welcome luxury. The building also had a huge backyard where children could play. The added bonus of my mother's sister and husband living in the same building seemed a miracle. My parents had achieved the American dream; they had finally found a safe, comfortable, and quiet place to raise a family.

Most of the apartment buildings and homes were built in the early 1900s. The first residents who occupied the apartments were new immigrants, Europeans, primarily from Ireland, with a few Italians arriving later. By the early 1930s, the migration of blacks from the South edged further and further into the city. Moving from the predominantly black West Side of Chicago, they found a home on the South Side where there were plenty of apartments to rent. When whites fled the area, black families filled the void.

Our apartment at 6425 S. Vernon was the center of our world, because we had cousins and friends who also lived in the building. We all played together, in the yards and on the porches. Our rectangular-shaped backyard lost every blade of grass to our trampling feet. On one side of the yard was Mrs. Lee's well-kept lawn, separated from ours by a picket fence. Any wayward ball that flew into that yard was considered gone forever. Mrs. Lee was very old and never saw a kid she liked. She was surprisingly vigilant and would spring into action whenever any errant ball found its way into her yard. Our secret name for her was Mrs. Peepee. She earned that name legitimately. The older kids always left her a wet front porch as a yearly Halloween gift.

The other side of the backyard was the back wall of the apartment building that was attached to ours. The buildings all had back porches onto which the back doors of the apartments led. At the very back of the yard was an old rickety wooden fence. Just inside the fence was a small patch of weeds where the local dogs found relief. The alley that ran behind the yard was paved. When rain fell heavily on summer days, the alley served well as a fast-running river for our little boats made from Popsicle sticks. Across the alley were the garages and backyards of apartment buildings that were located on the next street, Eberhardt. The alley was the main thoroughfare to and from school.

Kick the can, red light green light, hide and seek baseball, pick-up sticks, jacks, tag, jump rope, hopscotch, and running bases. The alley and the backyards were our playgrounds. The neighborhood's young knew the topography and niches well, all the best hiding places, and which shortcuts through tiny backyards were the best. We knew where the mean dogs were and which backyard had the best tomato gardens. We were not above a free tomato now and then.

All the nuances of any neighborhood in any city in America are learned from the vantage point of about four feet. I reached that height during the summer of 1954. I was going into the fourth grade and at nine years old, I was now old enough to go the store by myself. Freedom was Mr. Hamilton's grocery store. It was located on the block of 64th and Eberhardt, the next street over. The way to Mr. Hamilton's was through the backyard, down and across the alley, and through another backyard. The store faced Eberhardt Ave. A big plate-glass window with the words "Hamilton's Groceries" was painted in big red letters across the front.

This family business was simple and was like many small grocery stores around the country. It had wooden floors with a single aisle that went to the rear of the store. The aisle was about seven feet wide, formed by display cases that ran on either side; most had glass fronts. Shelves behind the cases held all the canned goods. From the level of four feet, everything seemed huge. Hanging from hooks behind the display cases like Christmas decorations were sausages and hotdogs. Meats and cheeses were in refrigerated cases. Behind all of this were Mr. and Mrs. Hamilton, the proprietors. She was as kind and gentle as he was grumpy.

To us, the most important part of the store was the candy section. This display case held every kind of candy a child could want. Licorice sticks, lollipops, Mary Janes, jawbreakers, juju bees, and packets of baseball cards. A cornucopia of delights.

"Artie."

I could hear Mom's call. I was on the back porch watching our neighbors, Bickey and Donnie, and my cousins Mickey and Jeff, playing Red Barber baseball. It was a board game that required dice and little pegs representing the ball players that you moved around the baseball diamond pictured on the board. Bickey, whose backdoor opened onto the porch, was a meticulous teenager who kept the game. He had statistics on every game the bigger kids played. Little notebooks with statistics were spread around.

Mickey had just thrown the dice and was screaming, "Six!!" The first die was thrown.

"Sixty!!!" The second die rolled on the board. Everyone was excited, because if he threw another six, he would have a home run and would win the game.

It was at this critical moment that Mom called.

"Artie!" Mom's second call.

"Yeah, Ma. I'm coming!"

"SIXXXXXXXX!!!!!!!!" Mickey went nuts. "Two months, two months I've been waiting to kick your butt, Bickey. Yahooooo!!!!!"

My cousin was a great kid. He lost every board game the big kids played, but he was always one of my favorites. Mickey was five years older than me, but was always fun. He was a really nice-looking youngster with straight black hair and long eyelashes. As one of the older boys in our building, he was our protector when Carol wasn't around.

"Artie, I'm not going to call you again!"

"OK, Mom. I'm sorry, but Mickey had a six, sixty, six!"

"A what?" Mom didn't know what in the world I was talking about.

"Mom, a six, sixty, six. A homer, in Red Barber," Mom wasn't very interested in baseball.

"OK. Fine. Honey, can you go to the store for me? I need some bologna for your dad's lunch for tomorrow."

I was staggered. My whole life was focused on getting bigger. Everything I could achieve would occur when that happened. Finally, here I stood. The words, the magical words, came from my mother's lips.

"Artie, can you go to the store for me?"

No longer was it, "Artie, Pete's going to the store. Why don't you go with him to help carry the groceries?" This was it. I was big.

"Sure, Mom. Happy to." I couldn't let on that this was new. She might change her mind. I was big for the first time. I meant to keep it.

"Whatcha need?"

"As I said, I need some lunch meat for your dad's lunch." A faint smile crossed her face.

I thought I'd venture a little into my new status.

"Should I get Marty to come help carry the stuff?"

Mom, who was standing at the kitchen sink, looked out the window over the sink and hid a little giggle.

"No, honey, I think you can carry the groceries all by yourself. After all, you're a teenager now, right?"

Amused, she continued, "I need a pound of sliced bologna and a loaf of bread."

"Tip Top bread!" I needed Mom to know I was a keen observer of our family's dining habits and the kind of bread Dad liked

"Yes, honey, that will be fine. Here's 50 cents. Tell Mr. Hamilton that I said to take the slices of bologna from the center. I don't want any end slices."

This was important information. I was not going to mess up my first instructions.

"Sure thing, Mom."

I walked out of the back door, which led from the kitchen. Mickey was still celebrating.

"Bickey, I just kicked your butt. I bet it hurts." Mickey was jubilant. "Is it cracked?" With that, Mickey let go with a howl. "Ha, ha, ha, haooooooooooo." It was a full minute before his laughter began to wane.

I waited for the guys to settle down. I was big now, and all the older guys needed to know that I was now part of their group.

"Yea, yea. One out of a thousand doesn't mean you'll ever win again," Bickey retorted.

"We'll see." Mickey was bold in his victory.

"Hey, fellas, I'm runnin' to the store, my mom needs some stuff. You guys need some candy?"

I figured they would really be impressed and immediately welcome me into the big boy's group.

"You going to the store alone?" Mickey looked over at me.

"Yeah, I am. Need something?" I answered

"Cool, daddio. Naw, I don't need anything." He winked at me.

"Make sure ole Hambone Chicken n' Gravy doesn't cheat you." Mickey laughed.

Hambone Chicken n' Gravy was Mr. Hamilton's nickname. No one knew how it came about, but that was it. Ole Hambone Chicken n 'Gravy.

"God, I love my cousin," I thought to myself. He knew. He realized what had happened. I was big.

"OK. Mick, how about you cats?"

"Naw, not me." "Me neither." The other fellas chorused.

"All right, fellas, I'll see you cats later." I had heard my cousin Jeff call his friends cat or cats, so since I was big now, I knew that I could say it, too.

I headed down the stairs, skipping every other step as I had seen Mickey, Jeff, and Pete do. I was big, finally.

In the backyard, Marty and Billy were playing catch with an old rubber ball. Billy was Mickey's youngest brother. He and Marty were about the same age and had a very close bond.

"Hey, Marty, you and Billy better be careful. Ole Mrs. Peepee is gonna have another one."

"Uh-uhhh, she ain't getting this one." Billy was certain.

"She sure ain't," Marty echoed. "If she tries, we'll run all the way around the block. She will never catch us."

"You better watch it anyway."

"Yea, she can run real fast." Billy had heard the story about Mrs. Lee. Some of us had even seen her run.

"You want to play catch with us?"

Billy loved playing catch. Rarely was he without some kind of a ball. Throwing it, catching it, bouncing it, it didn't seem to matter. He just loved playing with a ball, particularly catch. Like many of the kids in the neighborhood, he pretended to be either Pee Wee Reese, or Jackie Robinson. Pretending as if he was in a real game, making double plays or spectacular catches during a make-believe world series. He would always do the commentating while he played his made-up game.

"Ground ball up the middle. Caught by Billy. Steps on second. Over to Marty at first. And the runner is OOUUTTT for a double play, and the Cubs win the World Series. Yeaaaaa."

All of our games were played on a global stage.

This time though, they were only bouncing the ball against a wall when Billy asked if I wanted to play.

I, of course, was on more important business.

"Nah. I'm going to the store. I mean, I'm going to Hambone Chicken n' Gravy's to buy me some candy." I couldn't help but brag with a little lie attached.

"Ohhh, I'm telling!" Marty was the head tattletale in our family.

"I don't care if you do. Mom already knows. She asked me to go!" I was triumphant.

"I double-don't care. I'm still telling," Marty replied.

"Go ahead, you big tattle-telling baby." I answered. It was good to get in the last word.

I turned and proudly sauntered out of the backyard, their game of catch temporarily halted. When I snuck a peek back, I saw they were watching me, their mouths open in disbelief. A feeling of pride came over me. I was a big kid, and it was wonderful.

Out of the yard, I turned and headed toward Mr. Hamilton's store. My walking turned to skipping and then a big boy's full gallop. Jumped over cans and broken bottles. Past the telephone post that always smelled of urine. It was where the local winos urinated when they couldn't make it to an empty lot. The adults in the neighborhood were always furious with these tattered men. The kids, however, had fun with them and had devised names for them. There was Two Shoes Shortie because he was short and wore two different-colored shoes. Another one was Ole Punkin' Head. He had a giant head on a small skinny body. There was also a real crazy guy, Cross-eyed Charlie. He wandered through the streets, his eyes always rolling around and around while he swatted at imaginary bugs that seemed to be crawling in and out of his clothes.

You'd see these men in the alleys, a half-empty wine bottle nestled in a tattered back pocket. Their nightly travels were a mystery, but during the day they maneuvered the alleys and backyards as if the neighborhood streets were their living rooms. For too many, too often, this was true.

None of us were ever really afraid of them. They kept to themselves, trying to make it from day to day. Their concerns focused on how to get enough money for another bottle of Wild Irish Rose, or Muscatel, Thunderbird—it didn't seem to matter. Most of the adults in the neighborhood tolerated their presence, almost as if they were in need of protection. However, if they were ever disruptive or drunk in front of anyone's house, all kinds of hell would break loose. I remember Mrs. Lee chasing ole Cross-eyed Charlie down the street with a broom after he had urinated in front of her house.

She must have been keeping a neighborhood watch from her front window, because she came running out of her front door like a mad woman, screaming at the top of her lungs.

"Chaaallliieeeee geett yourrr butttttt outttaa hererere!!!"

Cross-eyed Charlie came out of his stupor, gathered his shaky legs beneath him, and took off, Mrs. Lee in hot pursuit. Every few feet she'd scream, "Come here! I'm a get you! I'm a get you! I'm a get you!"

She swung that old broom at him—swoosh—"I'm a get you"—swoosh.

Ole Cross eyed Charlie yelled "Yeeooooww!" the whole time.

Down our street they went, all the way to the end of the street, then around the corner, Mrs. Lee pursuing her half-drunken prey. He hadn't even had time to pull up his tattered pants.

"Come here! I'm a get you!"—swoosh—"Yeeeooowww!"—"Come here, I'm a get you!"—swoosh—"Yeeeooowww!"

No one had known how that old woman could run. There she was running down the street, a broom high in the air as she took massive swings at a fleeing Cross-eyed Charlie, her housecoat open, all kinds of fat falling out from the top of her rolled down stockings and from her floppy arms. Her eyes were fierce; she had tightly curled hair that swung from side to side with each massive step. Her house shoes had flown off, and her huge stomach bounced all over the place. There was a new respect for her because she was fast. It was the funniest thing I had ever seen. My cousin Jeffrey loved talking about it.

"If Ole Charlie woulda been hit by one of them giant bosoms, it would have knocked his eyes straight. Plus he had left his pants down, so he was running like a drunk penguin."

Jeffrey was on the back porch, telling that story to all the older boys one night. His eyes sparkled as he told the tale.

Our back porch was a gathering place for the kids in the neighborhood. We sat around glowing candles placed on old wooden milk crates that illuminated those summer nights. We listened to one another tell fantastic tales of high adventure. Stories drifting through warm summer evenings spoke to our imaginations. Sitting on that back porch listening and laughing, we could see beyond the boundaries of our neighborhood. I loved those soft nights and never wanted them to end.

As I ran down the alley to the store, I saw Jackie, a boy who lived down the block, and a couple of kids I had seen around but didn't really know looking into a garage. They were speaking conspiratorially, their heads close together as they peered into the garage. The big doors were pulled open; it must not have been locked.

As I got closer to the garage, I slowed down and walked up to them. I tip-toed behind them, trying to see what was happening in the garage. They were so engrossed in what they were doing they had not heard me walk up.

"Hey, what are you guys looking at?"

Their heads quickly turned toward me. Jackie even jumped a little bit when he heard my voice.

"Nothin'. Nothin'." The words came too quickly—in fact, before the guys even saw me.

"Oh, hey, Artie" Jackie, calming down, smiled at me, although he was still a bit nervous.

"It's just an old car. Where you goin?"

"To Mr. Hamilton's. I mean, ole Hambone Chicken n' Gravy's."

"Oh yeah? Getting some candy?" Jackie asked.

Jackie didn't have a father and his mom, we had figured out, didn't have any money cause we always gave them clothes and some of our old toys. We didn't feel sorry for him at all. My cousins and brother always avoided him when they were going to the store to buy candy. All the kids were willing to share their clothes, but important stuff like candy was a different matter.

"Naw, just some stuff for my dad."

I had purposely used my father's name to let Jackie know that this was a serious matter. I was going on an errand for my dad. It wasn't really a lie. My father was the person who needed the meat and bread.

"What are you guys doing? What's in there?" I asked as I edged closer to the opened doors of the garage.

"Nothin'. It's just an old car. We're not doin' anything wrong. You just go on to the store for your daddy!!"

Jackie blocked my view as he stepped in front of the garage. The word "daddy" was said with a lisp. Somehow, he was angry, and I knew enough to get out of there.

"OK. See ya." I quickly left.

I looked back as I neared the corner of the building that housed the store. I didn't see Jackie or the other boys. They had disappeared into the darkness of the garage. I watched as the doors closed, someone from inside the garage dragged them shut. I wasn't sure what was going on, but it couldn't have been good.

I turned away, my mission on my mind. I walked around to the front of the store and there it was, the entrance to Mr. Hamilton's. The smell of sawdust, pickles, assorted meats and vegetables met me. I pushed open the screen door with the advertisement to "Buy Pepsi" and the little bell rang as I stepped in. The door slammed behind me, ringing the little bell again. It was rigged so that it clanged when the screen door opened and shut. I stood in the entrance for a second. For the first time in my life, I was in the store by myself, my mom's money in my pocket.

Mr. Hamilton turned around and peered at me over his glasses. He turned back to the butcher's counter as the shrill of a meat slicer cut through the air.

SHHRRRREEEEEEEEEEE!

Mr. Hamilton hadn't said anything, so I decided to wait until he finished.

SSSSHHHHRRRREEEEEEE, SSSSSHHHHRRRREEEEE! SSSSSSHHHHHRRREEEEEEEE!

21

My patience drew thin, so I yelled over the sound of the machine.

"Mr. Hamilton. Mr. Hamilton! Mr. Hamiltonnnnn!!!"

I was a boy on a mission, sent to "bring home the bacon," one of my mom's favorite expressions. I had waited long enough. So I bellowed again with all the gusto a nine year old could muster.

"Mr. Hamiltonnnnn!!"

SSSHHHRREEEE. Click. Click. Phreewww. The machine ground to a halt.

"What do you want, boy?" he asked, clearly a bit annoyed.

Mr. Hamilton wore an apron around his ample belly. Small streaks of browned blood on his apron attested to his butchering skills. He was a short man with a small tuft of white, kinky hair that flared out from around the edge of the dirty paper hat he wore on his head.

"I need a pound of bologna and a loaf of bread, Tip Top bread."

I was a boy who understood his responsibilities.

"I don't want any end pieces on that bologna, either."

Is that so?" Mr. Hamilton replied. "And who taught you to talk to adults like that? I know your mother and father didn't."

Caught. Mr. Hamilton had invoked the dirtiest trick a nonparent could use, that of parental teaching. There was no answer. If I said my parents did teach me to speak like that, I was betraying my parents. If I said my parents didn't teach me to talk like that, then I was still wrong. My only choice was to apologize.

"I'm sorry. I mean, my mom said for you not to give me any end slices, please." I managed to save a little dignity.

"You better watch yourself, or you'll find yourself lying among the sweet peas."

This "sweet peas" thing was a normal threat by Mr. Hamilton. I had no idea what it meant, but it was something he often used when threatening the kids in the neighborhood.

"I'll cut it from the middle. How much do you want?"

"A pound of bologna and some bread, Tip Top" I said.

I turned to look at the candy as the shrill of the cutting machine again sliced though the air.

S H H H H H H R R R R R R E E E E E E E E E E E E E ! ! !
SHHHHHRRRREEEEEEE!!

I walked over to the low shelf where the bread was neatly dis-
played, picked up the Tip Top, and turned to the counter as Mr.
Hamilton finished.

"Here ya go." He pushed the buttons on his cash register, and I
saw the price on the machine.

"Let's see. One pound of sliced bologna. That's 30 cents. And a
loaf of bread."

He peeked over his glasses as he intoned with much grandeur,
"Tip Top bread."

"Let's see here." He mumbled a bit to himself. As he punched
the keys of the cash register, little numbers sprang up, assuring each
purchaser that the right price was being charged. A little bell rang at
the same time the keys were pressed.

"The bread is 13 cents." Ching-ching, "Plus tax of 1 cent." Ching-
ching. "OK, 44 cents, please."

I gave Mr. Hamilton the 50 cents Mom had given me.

"You want any candy? You got some change coming."

"No, sir, just that stuff." I knew better than to get anything without asking.

Mr. Hamilton handed the bag of groceries to me. The bread and
the bologna, wrapped in clean white paper and tied with a brown
string, were both neatly tucked into a paper bag.

I walked out of the store. The bell clanged as I let the screen
door slam. My mission was accomplished and I had remembered
everything. I felt the six cents change in my pocket. I was proud of
myself.

As I rounded the corner to go down the alley to get home, Jackie
and the other boys came running in my direction.

The three of them were moving fast, tight grins on their faces.
Every couple steps, they looked back as if someone or something was
coming after them. Two of them were bigger than me and one was
about my size. They came flying at me, yelling.

"Look out. Move! Move!"

They were screaming for me to get out of their way. I was frozen in place, unable to move. The path I was standing in was between two buildings and was only five feet wide. I was in their way and the way was narrow. I stared as they came at me, their arms pumping, feet slapping the pavement. I could hear them gasp for air, see their eyes wide with excitement as they barreled for me.

At the last instant, I was able to duck out of the way. As they passed I realized they had come running from the garage. I turned and watched as they got to the corner. They were moving quickly. As they disappeared around the corner, the last one, the one my size, glanced back at me. He looked like he was crying.

I picked up the groceries that I had dropped. My heart was beating quickly in my chest, I could feel the blood pumping in my temples. They had frightened me. I took a deep breath and headed home. When I passed the garage, I noticed that its doors were open. Something had gone on inside the little wooden building.

I was still unnerved. As I got closer to the garage, another feeling crawled into me, and it was fear. Yet somehow, I was drawn curiously to the almost-closed doors of the wooden garage. My nine-year-old mind was racing. What could have happened in there? Shaking slightly, I approached the huge wooden doors. Only one of them was open, that just barely. I looked in, there was only darkness. I put the groceries down and tugged on the door to let some daylight in. The afternoon light slowly crept into the garage as I strained to get it open. The bottom of the door ground against the concrete apron. I saw the front fender of an old car, nothing was wrong. I pulled the door harder as light flooded the garage. Shards of light reflected off the floor. Glass…broken glass was everywhere. The windows of the old car were shattered. Big rocks were on its front hood. It had to have been Jackie and those other kids.

Boy, would they be in trouble if anyone found out. I stepped out of the garage, picked up the groceries, and ran home. I had to find somebody to talk to. I needed to find out what I should do. If only I could find Carol or Pete, or one of my older cousins.

I ran to the backyard and up the back stairs. No one was there. Evidently, Mickey's six-sixty-six ended the afternoon's game.

"Artie, is that you?"

It was Mom.

"Yeah, it's me."

"Excuse me. 'Yeah?'" Mom required enunciation of every word.

"Sorry, yes, it's me."

"Did you get everything?" she inquired.

"Uh huh. I mean, yes, Mom." I was out of breath and it was hard to hide it.

"Artie? You OK? You sound out of breath." She opened the screen door to let me in.

"I was just trying to hurry up," I lied.

"MMMM OK. Put the meat in the icebox and the bread in the breadbox. Fold the paper bag up and put it on the stack of paper in the pantry."

"OK."

I was still a bit nervous. None of my siblings were home. I had to talk to someone.

Maybe Mom. I quickly decided against that. She would have made me go back and clean up the garage and let the people who owned the garage and the car know what happened. I was afraid they would blame me. I was scared.

As I quickly put the stuff away, I headed for the back door.

"Artie?" Mom again.

"Yes, Mom?"

"Didn't you forget something?"

"Huh? No, I got everything" She must have somehow found out what had happened.

"Think about it." She crossed her arms and looked down at me. She knew, but how? Her finger tapped on her chin as she held her arms across her chest.

"What, Mom?" I wasn't going to give in easily. Heck, it wasn't my fault. I didn't do anything wrong.

"Artie?" She hesitated.

I was about to cave in. I couldn't take the pressure.

"It wasn't me!" The words came out of my mouth at the same time she said, "What about the change?"

"Oh, yes, the change. I almost forgot." I quickly fished the six cents from my pocket and handed it to her, all the time hoping she hadn't heard what I had said.

"What did you say?" Mom hadn't missed it.

"Huh? Oh, I was saying 'Excuse me.' I burped."

"Sure you did."

Mom wasn't convinced, but I hoped she'd let it go.

"I'm going outside." I said as I headed out the door. I was still desperate to tell someone about the garage and the car.

"No. Dinner is almost ready, so I want you to set the table. I just sent Marty out to get your brother and sister. You go to the bathroom and wash up first, using soap this time, and then set the table. By the way, I still want to know why you said 'It wasn't me.' We'll talk after dinner."

I walked into the bathroom to wash my hands. I was caught. There was no way to get around what I had witnessed. Somehow, I was going to have to explain why I didn't try to stop the other boys. I knew that even if I didn't break anything, I was still responsible. In our neighborhood, if you saw it, you did it. Tough rules, but it put pressure on all the kids to report any misbehavior.

After I set the table, my brothers and sister came home. Dad had been in all afternoon. He usually got home early. As a milkman he left home before dawn but got home before 3:00 p.m. and then took a nap.

Our dinners were always noisy. My parents sat quietly as their children competed for attention. If the story we had for the day's activities was dull, we would create a more exciting story; swearing the adventure to be true. As my family talked enjoying our family ritual, I sat quietly, unnerved by what had happened earlier.

My mother, while looking at me, spoke to my father:

"How was work today, Warren?" She moved her gaze to Dad, who sat at the head of the table.

"Fine, nothing unusual."

My father was a man of few words.

Mom looked back at me, hesitated a moment, then, "Artie, you're mighty quiet this evening. Why is that....?

The phone rang, saving me. BRRRIIIIIINNNNGG! BBRRRRIIIIINNNNGGG!

Carol got up.

"Artie." Mom was still looking at me.

"Mom! It's for you," my sister called from the hallway where the phone was.

A moment's respite. Mom got up, still looking at me.

"Hello? Yes, this is Mrs. Miller. Yes. Yes. What? Mr. Malarcher's garage? What time did it happen? Who saw him? His car, too? How bad was it? Who else? Saw him running away, huh? How many? Well, thank you, Mrs. Lee. I appreciate the call...Ha. Ha.. No, we won't. Bye . OK. Bye now."

Mom came back to the table.

"What was that all about?" Dad asked.

"Well, it seems that our middle son had a real adventure today," she replied.

"I don't understand. What are you talking about? What adventure? Artie, what is your mother talking about?"

Dad looked at me as he lowered the fork in his hand. His hard hand wiped across his mouth.

There I was. I began to explain, but the tears started.

"I was going to the store for Mom," sniff, sniff, "just like you to.. tol..told me, Mom."

The tears were flowing now.

"I was going to the store to get some Tip Top bread and bologna, and I saw some boys at the garage down the alley. I think they broke the windows in a car that was in there. I looked in the garage when I was coming home and saw all the glass, but I didn't do anything, I promise, I didn't do it!"

"What boys?" Dad wasn't playing.

The glare of my father was such that any thought of protecting Jackie and the other boys was nonexistent.

"It was Jackie and some other boys who live down the street."

"Helen, get on the phone and round up those other boys. Tell their parents I'll meet them at Malarcher's house." He then snatched me out of my seat and said, "C'mon, boy. Time to face the music! I'm telling you right now, if you lied to me or if you broke anything, you will get the whipping of your life. Do you understand me?"

I got it. There was one thing that was known in my house. If you messed up, you paid for it. Period.

My brothers and sister were so scooted down in their chairs, all you could see were their hands as they ate dinner. Around the table little hands reached for food, then disappeared into heads bent low to the table.

I didn't finish dinner that evening.

Mr. Malarcher's house was about 200 feet down the block. His home was beautifully maintained. The building was of brick construction. Sandy brown bricks were used on the back and sides of his two-story home. The bricks on the front of the house facing the street were a reddish brown. The top edge of the building facing the street was made with concrete and had designs that looked like shells from giant snails.

His home sat behind a chained fence about three feet high painted green. The fence completely encircled his property. Beside his neat home was a lawn with perfectly placed trees and flowers. His was the only manicured lawn on the block, a tiny oasis amid the trampling, grass-killing feet of little children.

Dad had me by the back of my shirt. I could feel his knuckles bang against the back of my head as he nearly dragged me down the street. When we passed Mrs. Lee's house, I could see her standing on her porch, smiling.

"OK, knucklehead, who else was with you? And you better not lie to me!"

Dad was not happy.

There was no question that in the face of this terror, I would have divulged every secret I had ever known. But, I just couldn't remember the other boys' names.

"Dad, I...I... pro..." I couldn't talk because on every step, Dad's knuckles banged into the back of my head.

"I promise... I told...tol.. you..the ..tru..tru..truuth."

The back of my head had little knots on it when we finally made it to Mr. Malarcher's house. Dad pushed opened the gate that entered into his front yard. We climbed the front stairs that were flanked by several huge pots that had flowers with huge blossoms spilling out.

A massive wooden door stood in front of us. Large, ornate hinges held the door in place. At chest level was a brass knocker. A small, four-pane window with a tiny sheer curtain just above the knocker hid prying eyes from seeing into the house. The sun was slowly settling into the evening sky, so the door was half in shade and half in sunlight.

CLANG, CLANG, CLANG!!!!

My father let go of my shirt. I readjusted it so the top button wasn't against my throat.

He was about to grab the brass knocker again when the door opened.

Warren and Helen Miller circa 1954

Chapter three

Grown Folks

"Hello, David." My father was uncomfortable. A proud man, I had never witnessed him in a subservient role.

"Hello, Warren." Mr. Malarcher was about my father's size, 5'7", thin and athletic.

"Come on in." He stepped aside, allowing us to enter. My father's hands were on my shoulders. It was strange that I felt safe under his hands, considering the pain in the back of my head.

The smell of the house is what I noticed first. It smelled like the library. I could imagine the rows of books that stretched to the ceiling in the library on 63rd St. with its tall bookshelves burdened by enormous books, row upon row of books. Everything was orderly in Mr. Malarcher's house. It was as neat and clean as his front yard. There were built-in cabinets on the far wall of his living room, and a brick fireplace stood in the center of the opposite wall. Over the fireplace was a mantel that held several trophies with little baseball players on top. Also on the mantel were about a dozen baseballs on metal stands. A picture of a young family, a father, wife, and several kids, hung over the fireplace.

Lamps with green shades that had fringes of a darker green stood on two tables that were next to two large leather chairs. Several books

31

were on the table next to one of the chairs. They faced a huge brown couch. Separating the couch from the chairs was a coffee table with more books and magazines carefully stacked in the middle.

The room was clean and neat. On the couch sat Jackie and his mom.

My dad spoke to Jackie's mom.

"Hi, Ellen. Considering the circumstances, it's nice to see you."

"Helllooo, Warren." Jackie's mom was looking strangely at my father.

Another of the boys was on a chair near the wall. I knew him only as bald-headed Bobby. He was alone. Often, we saw him around our block with Jackie. They were similar in appearance, a bit tattered with holes in their pants. You could always see new patches sewn on the old patches that covered the holes. All of us had a patch here and there on our clothing, but they had patches on patches. Their whole corduroy pants were patches.

As the middle of three sons, I knew about patches. I wore the hand-me-downs that I inherited from my brother and cousins, and they were always pretty rough on their clothes.

"You're Mamie Till, aren't you?" Dad spoke to the other woman sitting on the couch. The boy next to her must have been her son. I remembered him as one of the other kids at the garage.

"Yes, you're Mr. Miller?" She was formal. Her son was looking at the floor; his shoulders slumped forward, as if he were studying a pattern in the rug beneath his feet.

"This is my son, Emmett."

"I see." Dad looked around, nudged me toward a chair, then stood behind me, his hands on the back of the chair. Then, uncharacteristically, he moved his hands onto my shoulders.

Mr. Malarcher cleared his voice. "Uhhhmm, I had a visitor this afternoon, I don't want to say whom. This ...visitor said there were some youngsters running down the alley after coming from my garage. It was suggested that I look to see why they were in my garage. So I went to the back there, and, frankly, it hurt. It hurt to see what these kids did. What I discovered was disturbing and hurtful. I found that large rocks shattered the windows in one of my cars, apparently. After a phone call or two, I was able to figure out who the culprits were.

"If it's OK with you, I would ask that the boys tell us what happened." This last comment was directed to the parents in the room.

"OK, who wants to go first?" Mr. Malarcher spoke in a clipped style. Each word started and ended quickly, as if the words were exploding out of his mouth. "OK...WHO...WANTS...?"

"I will." Jackie bravely began. I relaxed a little. I could feel my father's hand tense a bit. He didn't have to worry. I wasn't going anywhere.

"We were just foolin' around. We didn't think that ole car was any good." Jackie was talking fast, like he always did. It was as if he thought if he talked fast enough, no one could disagree or argue with him.

"It wasn't a new car and it was all dusty and dirty, and stuff. Besides, the tires were flat. Ain't nobody been driving it."

Jackie's mom stiffened. My father's hands clinched in reaction to Jackie's explanation. It hurt. I thought, "Dad would have popped me upside the head for not admitting that I...we were wrong. Somebody say something, please!"

"Tweet, tweeeet, tweeet."

A twittering sound came from the couch. It was Emmett.

Emmett's mom looked at him. "You want to say something?"

I wondered why he was whistling. What in the heck was that all about? That would have garnered another pop upside the head from Dad.

"We... we...w.we we m... m... messed up." It was Emmett.

"You damned right you did." Dad reacted with his normal directness. Emmett's mom shot a glance at my father. I'd not witnessed anyone look at him in such a way. She clearly was not pleased with her son but was unwilling to allow anyone to answer for her child while in her presence. She looked at Emmett, who had dropped his head.

"Go on now. What else do you have to say?"

"Tweet, tweet... we w we I didn't realize th that I wa wa was do do.... I'm sorry."

Emmett's mom looked at him. "Yes you are. Emmett, you are going to have to pay Mr. Malarcher. All you boys are going to have to pay for the damage you've caused."

"Mr. Malarcher, what do you think it will cost to replace the windows for your car?" Mrs. Till was direct and calm.

"I have not contacted anyone as yet. I imagine it will be at least $30 to $35. I know that is a lot of money, but I believe I may have an idea."

Mr. Malarcher stood near his fireplace fingering one of the trophies on the mantel.

"They can do some yard work that needs to be done. I also would like to tell them…no, teach them about a few things."

I could feel my father's hands loosen their grip on my shoulders. They had tightened a bit when Mrs. Till spoke to him.

"That sounds like that's fair to me. There are only a few weeks left before their summer vacation will be over. I suggest they start tomorrow morning."

My dad was quick to try to regain his feeling of control. He continued, "Getting up early in the morning should do these boys some good!"

"Warren, if you don't mind, I would like to hear from each of the young men before we decide if this is what we're going to do."

My father slowly nodded in agreement. This was another man's home.

Mr. Malarcher was firm. While he was speaking to my father, he turned and looked at me.

"Your name is?" he asked, his eyes were hard to avoid. He was direct, yet… gentle... even kind.

"I'm Artie," I sort of mumbled.

"Artie... hmm. What do you have to say about my car and what happened?"

"I don't know."

"What do you mean?"

"I didn't hit your car. I just saw those guys running from your garage and then I looked inside and saw all the glass and the rocks, and stuff. And, I just grabbed the bologna and Tip Top bread and ran home and couldn't find anybody. And I didn't tell my mom and dad, and …"

"Whoa. Slow down. We aren't in a hurry. Now, you said that you didn't throw anything at my car, is that right?"

"Uh huh. I mean, yes sir."

"I see."

With his eyes still on me, he spoke to my dad.

"Warren, do you think your son should be here?"

Mr. Malarcher had a curious smile on his face.

I could feel my father move a little behind me. His hands, however, never left my shoulders. I was glad he was still there.

He hesitated a moment, then started.

"This neighborhood has to watch out for itself. If it doesn't, no one else will, that's for sure. This boy should have first told us about what happened; he knows that. My wife and I have taught our kids to be responsible. So, he will pay the price for not doing what he knows he's supposed to do."

My dad was absolutely convinced, as were the rest of the grown-ups that everyone in the neighborhood had to live well together or they would live poorly together. It was constantly driven into our heads about loving thy neighbor and all that stuff.

Mr. Malarcher accepted my father's statement. Obviously, he was in complete agreement. He looked around at the boys huddled in their seats. He was a little less direct as he spoke to the one boy there whose parents weren't present.

"Bobby, I spoke with your mom. She said that you have a job as a paperboy. Is that right?"

"Yes, sir." Bald-headed Bobby didn't move.

His hands were clasped together, his feet tucked beneath the chair, the tips of his dirty Buster Brown's barely touching the carpet beneath his feet as they nervously swayed back and forth, back and forth.

"I make $2.00 a week; I got $7.57 saved up."

He looked up, his eyes red as a swelling under one eye showed a purplish hue.

"My mom lets me spend 25 cents a week for candy. I have to pay her $1 and the rest I have to save. She told me I had to give you my candy money, if that's OK?"

He finished and sat back a bit. His feet came up off the floor.

Mr. Malarcher was silent a moment, then cleared his throat.

"Uhhhmm. Ok, Bobby, I want you to come over here and work with the other boys. Maybe we will work out a smaller payment, but I don't want you to have to give up your candy money. We'll make a different arrangement with you. Because you'll pay a little bit for the windows, we will make you the boss. I'll have you supervise your friends. You know, manage them and make sure they work hard. What do you think?"

"Huh.. Yea, I guess." Bobby seemed confused.

Mrs. Till and Jackie's mom hid soft smiles. I didn't understand all that was happening. I would ask my father later.

"How come he gets to be the boss?" Jackie, again with his big mouth. Before anyone could move, his mom popped him upside his head.

Whap!

"Dang, Ma, why'd you do that?" Jackie said while he rubbed the back of his head.

"Boy, wait'll I get your butt home." Him mom wasn't playing.

"I shoulda been the boss." Jackie murmured. Boy just wouldn't shut up.

"My son will be here whenever you require him to be. If he does anything wrong, you can let me know. I am sick and tired of this boy getting into trouble all the time. I don't know what I'm going to do with him."

Jackie's mom seemed to be speaking to everyone, but to no one.

"I swear, one of these days...."

Mr. Malarcher interrupted her.

"I believe that Jackie and I will get along fine. Don't you think so, Jackie?" The last words were spoken as if someone had squeezed his throat. His teeth were slightly clenched, and you could see spit fly from his lips. His brow had moved down, hooding his eyes.

Jackie got the message. "Uh, yea. I guess so."

"Good. Now that we are all in agreement.... Today is Friday, and school begins in two weeks. Let's see...."

Mr. Malarcher walked over to the desk that sat in the corner of the living room.

"I believe if you boys were to come over to the house beginning tomorrow, which is Saturday."

The last few words he spoke as if to himself, one hand on his chin, the other on a pair of wire-rimmed glasses he had picked up.

"If you were to be here at, let's say, 8:00 a.m. and worked until 12:00 or 1:00 every day except Sunday; you should be able to finish the work that needs to be done."

He stopped and waited for a reply.

The adults, as if one, answered, "Yea." "No problem." "Sounds good."

The boys responded as one. "Huh." "Dog gone." "Shoot. That ain't fa...."

Whap! Jackie's mom went upside his head again.

"It is fair, you little knuckleheaded sonofa...."

Mr. Malarcher seemed to be at a loss. He shook his head slightly before he spoke.

"Well, boys, you go on home. I would like to speak to your parents alone, if it's OK with them."

He looked at the adults for approval. They all nodded, except my dad, who more or less shrugged his shoulders.

I got up as my father removed his hands from my shoulders. I walked to the front door with the other boys. As we filed out of the house, I looked back. They were not watching us. Mr. Malarcher was speaking to Jackie's mom. Mrs. Till was nodding as she reached over to touch her arm. My father hadn't moved, he stood apart from the rest, watching.

The sun was bright and I had to shield my eyes as we left the house. The four of us stood on the porch adjusting to the light. The sun was low enough in the sky for its rays to shine directly beneath the overhang that sheltered the front door of the house from the midday heat.

Jackie, of course, was the first to speak.

"Bobo, I almost peed my pants when you started that whistling, dodo."

"Ah, leave me alone. You know I get nervous sometimes," Emmett answered.

"Yea, but that was soooo..."

"Shut up, Jackie, or I'll kick your ugly black...."

Before Emmett could let loose with what would have been the juiciest bit of cussing I'd ever wanted to know, the sound of movement came from the house.

"I'm sure they'll learn their lesson." It was Mr. Malarcher. Then someone said something too softly to be understood.

In an effort to avoid confronting Emmett, Jackie lowered his voice and whispered, "And why did they make you the boss?"

Bald-headed Bobby shrugged his shoulders. "I dunno, I ...dunno."

I was ignored, which suited me. Not knowing what my position was with them, being left out was fine.

The sounds of footsteps and muffled voices came from inside the house.

"OK. Yes. 8:00 a.m. Well, I'm glad we've been able to discuss this. I'm sorry, Warren I didn't hear you. What was that you said? Yes, I did, about 25 years." It was Mr. Malarcher.

The adults appeared at the front door; Jackie's mom, Emmett's mom, and then my dad.

They nodded their good-byes, each leaving in different directions, except Bobby who walked with Emmett and his mom. They evidently lived near one another over on St. Lawrence Ave., a couple blocks over.

We walked toward home in silence, my father setting a fast pace; he kept just ahead of me.

He slowed after a moment and looked down at me.

"You don't know who he is, do you?"

"Mr. Malarcher?"

"Yes. You don't know who he is, do you?" He repeated the question, but this time he wasn't looking at me but had gone back to his quick pace toward home. His question was directed more to the empty air in front of him rather than to me.

"He played baseball in the Negro Leagues. I thought he had and I asked him when we left his house.

"He did, really?" I responded.

My father was a big fan of baseball and had played for the milk company he worked for, Hawthorne Melody. He was a second baseman and we often went to see him play. After his games he would talk about great "colored" ball players, "Cool Papa" Bell, Satchel Paige, Ted "Double Duty" Radcliffe. The players' names rolled from his lips like poetry. My brothers, sister, and I never tired of his stories about the ballplayers he so admired.

Some of the most exciting times in the community were when the Brooklyn Dodgers or the New York Giants came to Chicago to play the Cubs. On those days we all gathered around the radio to listen to Jack Brickhouse call the game.

Dad had an undying affection for the Cubs, however, he inevitably switched allegiances whenever his beloved Cubs played the Dodgers or the Giants. All anyone in the neighborhood would talk about were the Negro players on those two teams.

On the Giants were Henry Thompson and Monte Irvin, while Brooklyn had Roy Campanella, Don Newcombe, and Jackie Robinson, the first black baseball player in the Major leagues. He had been the rookie of the year and was a real source of pride for Negroes. Dad said he was the best player in baseball, and we believed him.

On the walk home I realized that I would get to be around someone my father looked up to. Maybe everything wouldn't be so bad after all.

Chapter four

Lessons Learned

"Artie. Artie. It's time to get up." It was Mom. "You go get washed up. I believe you have some work to do this morning, right? You don't want to be late. So go wash up, and make sure you use soap this time."

Mom was in the kitchen when she woke me up early on Saturday morning.

I rubbed my eyes and yawned. My brothers were still asleep. I could hear them as a soft drone rose from beneath the blankets next to me. Because there were three of us, someone had to sleep in the middle, or what we referred to as the "crack." Marty, the youngest, was usually bullied into that very uncomfortable spot. I slept next to the wall, and Pete slept on the other side. The three of us slept in the dining room on a hide-away bed. In the morning after everyone was awake, one of the beds easily collapsed and was rolled underneath the other. A slipcover was put on the remaining bed, and it made for a simple couch. This worked well if only two people slept in the beds, but ….

We believed the best and safest place to sleep was next to the wall, because we thought if there were any monsters in the house at night, they would begin by eating the brother on the end, then the brother next to him. But the one next to the wall wouldn't be eaten because the monsters would be full by then.

I sat up, two sleeping bodies curled next to me. Rather than exit the bed so as to not awaken my brothers, I crawled over them. It was important that they not sleep since I had to get up.

"Ooooppss. Sorry. Didn't mean to kick you, Pete."

"Aaaahhh, man. Mom, tell Artie to get off me." Pete's voice came from beneath the covers. His body was a lumpy ball; I couldn't see where his head was, since he was completely hidden beneath the blanket.

I wasn't sure where my knee had landed, but it met something soft. With a little moan, he moved. My knee had done the job. Pete was awake. Marty, however, just groaned and squirmed but didn't wake up.

I shuffled into the bathroom, as a sly smile on my face. I turned and watched as Pete slowly sat up and stared at me, thinking to myself, "What a nice morning." As I walked into the bathroom, I noticed there was no soap on the sink. Ah haa! Another opportunity to mess with my brothers presented itself. I couldn't resist.

"MOOOMMM! Where's the soap?!"

I heard Marty groan. "Ummmm, Maaa, tell Artie to shudup."

I hoped the "crack" was doing its work.

"MOOMMMM, where's the wash cloth!!!???!!!??" I yelled into the morning air.

"Artie, stop it!" Mom was right behind me.

She had quietly walked up and had scared the heck out of me.

"The soap and wash cloth are right there. Now you be quiet."

"OK. Sorry."

I quickly turned on the faucet, threw water on my face, and made noises like I was washing up. Peering into the circular mirror over the basin, I could see in its reflection the little metal tip on the string that hung from the single light bulb fastened to the ceiling. I watched as the string swung, left, right, left, right. I looked at my face. Frances, the pretty girl who lived on the first floor of our building with her sister and three brothers, had said I was "cute." I couldn't tell. But, hmmm. "Cute." I liked that. I wasn't sure what "cute" meant, but I was glad that she said I was.

41

"Yea, that's right. I'm cute." I whispered to myself.

"Artie! You hurry up in there. You will not be late this morning."

"OK, Mom. Almost done." I pulled the mirror open. Behind it was the medicine cabinet that revealed all the interesting and wonderful things I was never allowed to touch—smelly ointments, creams and lotions, razors and brushes, bandages—really great stuff. I peered at everything for a while, poking at jars, tubes, and little boxes.

"Artie!" Mom again.

"There. I'm all done, Ma," as I turned the faucet off.

I walked down the hallway through the dining room. My brothers were now awake, and they peered at me from the bed. As I passed them, I stuck my tongue out at them. They in turn, simultaneously pointed their fingers at me, wiggled them, and quietly said, "Nah-na-nah-na-nah-na-nah. You got to go to wooorrrrk."

This was all done with a little tune as they moved their necks from side to side.

I was then obliged to stick my tongue out even further. Unfortunately, I couldn't think of a quick retort. So I told on them.

"Mom, they're teasing me."

Unfortunately, Mom saw the whole thing.

"Boys...stop. Artie, just get in here."

I turned away from my brothers, but not before giving them one more good look at my tongue. They, in turn, crossed their eyes reached out their arms in an exaggerated stretch, and put their hands over their mouths to stifle fake yawns.

"Wow, Marty, you sleepy? Guess I'll sleep all day. No, maybe we'll play marbles while Artie's working. What do you think?"

Pete was ingenious in his teasing.

"Yea, maybe we'll play cards." Marty was warming up to the fun.

"Mom, they're still teasing me."

"Artie, if you leave them alone…. Boy, just get in here and eat your breakfast. You guys are going to be the death of me yet." Another of her favorite sayings.

I walked into the kitchen and sat at the little table in the corner across from where Mom was standing at the sink. She had gotten a bowl of cereal for me and milk from the icebox. I got a glass from the pantry and poured some milk to drink and for my cereal. I looked at "Snap, Crackle, and Pop" the characters on the Rice Krispies box. My brothers and I had assigned ourselves the role of each of the characters. Pete had selected "Pop," I was "Snap," and Marty was "Crackle." I stuck my tongue out at "Pop" and "Crackle." Mom turned from the sink, smiled at me, and said, "Artie, I am expecting you to work very hard at Mr. Malarcher's."

"I will, Mom. I promise." We were quiet a moment.

"Mom, I'm sorry I messed up. I don't know why I didn't tell you. Are you still mad at me?"

"Artie, sweetheart, I was never mad at you. Your father and I want you to understand that it is really important to tell us about everything that happens to you or anyone else. We never want you to get in trouble or get hurt. What we really need is for you and your brothers and sister to always believe that you can come and talk to us about everything. If you do that, then we can make certain you guys are always safe."

"I'm really sorry, Mom." I felt pretty badly about messing up.

"Honey, why didn't you tell us what happened? We would have made sure that everything would have been taken care of."

"I don't know, Mom, I guess I was scared."

"Scared? Scared of what?"

"I don't know, Mom. Just scared about what those boys had done, about them being in trouble. About what would happen…. Mom, I don't know… I'm not sure. Maybe I was scared of what would happen if I told on them."

"Artie, no matter what ever happens to you, or if you are afraid of something, or don't know what to do, please remember you can always, always come and tell me. OK?"

"OK, Mom, I am real, real sorry. I promise I will always tell you everything. OK? I really, really promise. Cross my heart. "

Invoking the "Cross my heart" promise and raising my right hand while crossing my heart with my left was proof positive of my sincerity.

"OK, honey. After you're done eating, I'll walk down to Mr. Malarcher's with you."

"Naw....Uh, I mean, no, that's OK. I can go by myself. Remember, I went to Mr. Hamilton's all by myself."

"Yes, you did. And you brought back everything perfectly. Even the Tip Top bread."

"Yep, I brought home the bacon." Mom loved to say, "You brought home the bacon." This somehow meant someone had done a good job.

She smiled at me. "Yes, you certainly did. You brought home the bacon."

"Yep. I'm all finished eating, so I'll see ya later, Ok?" I got up from the table and put the bowl and spoon in the sink. Mom kissed me on the forehead.

"Bye, honey. Be careful."

"I will." I said this as I walked toward the back door with an eye on my brothers' lumpy forms lying in the bed.

"Hey, Pete, Marty. I hope you guys smell each others feet and socks all day!"

I quickly ran out the back, letting the screen door slam behind me. I got out before they could say anything.

Running down the back stairs, I felt pretty good about teasing my brothers. I certainly felt better than I had when Dad and I got back from Mr. Malarcher's house the evening before. My siblings expressed a real interest in knowing what had happened and were particularly interested in the severity of the punishment I would face.

The moment we stepped through the front door, Carol teasingly inquired, "Hey, Dad, you want me to get your razor strap?" This was said with her hand over her mouth to hide her grin, but the look in her eyes gave her away.

Fortunately, my dad wasn't in a playful mood and ignored her.

He muttered something that reflected his mood.

"Damn, dumb, don't know diddly-squat about reality. You guys have a lot to learn yet. I hope your brother learns his lesson. He is going to have to work to help pay for the damage he and some other kids did."

"But, Dad, I didn't...."

"Boy, don't start with me. I thought I had made it clear you are responsible anytime you see someone do something they are not suppose to be doing and you decide not to tell us. Now that's it. Do you understand me?"

"Yes, sir. I understand."

That was the end of that conversation. Dad's glare meant the next one to speak would have been popped upside the head. So I shut up, as did my siblings.

Late that night, I explained to my brothers what had happened. They were quiet as I told them the story. They just listened, and that was good. We had a closeness that happens only when you spend every night in the same bed with each other, sometimes huddled against the cold, sometimes against the night. We deeply loved one another; and that night, as we had all of our lives, we fell asleep together.

Despite my deep affection for my brothers, teasing them this morning was deeply satisfying. It was a tradition that we embraced happily.

As I ran down the back steps, I heard someone talking. It was Frances, the cute girl who lived with her family on the first floor. Her voice drifted up to me as I slowed my run down the stairs. I hadn't seen her since my cousin Billy told me she thought I was cute. Even though I had known and seen her my entire life, for some crazy reason, I had butterflies in my stomach. I slowed down, hoping she would go away. I peeked around the banister from the first-floor landing and didn't see her. I hesitated a moment and considered going back upstairs to go down the front steps. Then realized I would have to face my brothers again. Facing her would be easier than being bothered by them. So I slowly walked down the stairs. She still wasn't there. I quietly edged down the stairs. I was about to get past the open door to their apartment when I heard, "Hi, Artie." I was caught.

"Oh, hi, Frances." I panicked. What should I do? Thoughts flooded my mind. I can't stop walking, I have to hurry up. Stop looking at my feet. Where else do I look. Hurry up! Get going! Don't fall down! Get going! Get going!

"Where you goin', to the store?" She asked.

"Uh-uhhh. Nah, I got to go to work," I lied.

"Mr. Malarcher's, huh?"

"Yes." Doggone it, everybody knew about what happened.

So, I did the best thing I could think of, the only option left to me. I acted forthrightly. I ran as fast as I could. Not a "see ya" or "bye" came out of my mouth. I just ran. I ran down the last few steps, through the backyard, and around to the front, just to get away from her. I didn't stop running until I got to the front gate of Mr. Malarcher's house.

I stood there, my hands on the gate. I needed a moment to catch my breath. The panic slowly gave way to calm. It was behind me. I was better.

"Whew." I didn't think or worry about what I would say to Frances the next time I saw her. All I knew was I didn't have to say anything to her then. That was one problem behind me.

I looked at the gate of the house in front of me. The butterflies I had run away from found me and brought most of their friends. They settled into their familiar place, the pit of my stomach, which received them hungrily.

I opened the gate and slowly walked up the steps to the front porch. The heavy wooden door was open, so I could hear some music coming from inside the house. It was the kind of music my parents listened to, jazz. I stood listening for a moment nervously, hoping that the other boys had gotten there before me. I felt the butterflies erupting into what must have been a butterfly war. I tried to think of what to do. Should I knock on the screen door, or should I go home and ask my mom to come back with me? As if I had come out of a fog, I realized that the only thing that separated me from the inside of Mr. Malarcher's house was a screen door. But somehow it didn't feel like a barrier, only a way to allow the morning air into the house. I felt safe. The butterflies stopped their skirmish.

With no door to knock on, I put my face against the screen and said, "Hello, Mr. Malarcher. It's me, Artie."

After a second he came to the entrance. He had on the same kind of overalls my dad wore for work. It startled me, because every time I had seen him before, he had been wearing a white shirt and tie. He looked neat and clean even in the overalls.

"Hello. Come on in."

He unlocked the screen door and opened it, then stepped back. As I walked in, I noticed the smell of books was still in the air.

"You're early. That's good. The others haven't gotten here yet. Artie?"

"Yes, sir?"

"How do you feel about having to work to pay for my car windows?"

"I don't know." I was not sure what to say. The best response was the always available, "I don't know."

Mr. Malarcher smiled. "Yea, I suppose it is hard to know why we do things and how we feel about them. You know, I used to say the same thing when I was a kid, 'I don't know.' It always seemed like the safest thing to say."

I liked Mr. Malarcher. He was talking to me like I was a grownup.

"Everyone on the block was surprised when they heard you were in trouble. Did you know that?"

"No, sir." I was unsure what I was supposed to say, but somehow "I don't know" didn't seem to work. Fortunately, there was a light rapping on the screen door. It was Bobby.

"Come on in. Good morning." Mr. Malarcher had turned and stepped toward the front door.

"Good morning, Mr. Malarcher." Bobby then looked at me and nodded.

"Have a seat, boys. We'll wait for your friends."

He turned and walked out of the room. We heard him turn on a faucet in the kitchen and then, drawers opening and closing. Bobby and I sat on the couch waiting, looking at each other, wondering what to do.

Bobby whispered, "Wow, look at all those baseballs and trophies and stuff. You think they're his?"

"I don't know, but there sure are a lot of them."

Bobby looked to see if Mr. Malarcher was still around before he got off the couch to take a closer look at the trophies. To get a good look, he had to grab the mantel and stand on his toes. Even on his toes, he could barely see. The mantel was about five feet from the floor.

"You better be careful, Bobby. You gonna break something."

"Wow…dag…man-o-man. Wow. Dig that."

I was so interested in watching Bobby; and Bobby was so busy trying to get a good look at the stuff on the mantel, that neither one of us heard Mr. Malarcher as he quietly came back into the room. I had already noticed his movements were almost soundless, as if his footsteps defied the physics of sound.

"Hmmm. Do you like those things?"

Bobby nearly knocked everything off the mantel trying to get back on the couch, while I nearly jumped out of my skin.

"No, it's OK. You can look at that all you want. Artie, you can take a look, too. You know what, better still, I'll take those things down so you can take a good look-see."

Bobby and I sat cross-legged on the floor as Mr. Malarcher brought down everything—all of the trophies and plaques and pictures—that was on the mantel. He then disappeared into a back room and brought out more things. In front of us were baseballs that someone had written on, trophies and plaques, pictures of baseball players, of entire teams, and some with one or two men in dirty uniforms holding baseball bats. Some photos had men wearing catcher's masks and some in crouched positions like they were getting ready to catch a ground ball.

"Mr. Malarcher, where'd you get all this stuff? My dad said you used to be a baseball player. Did you get it by playing baseball?"

"Yes, Artie, I used to be a baseball player, but that was when I was much younger. It was a very exciting and wonderful life. I played all over the country. I even went to foreign countries, too."

We heard Jackie and Emmett before they knocked. They were speaking softly, so we were unable to hear what they were saying, but we could hear them.

Tap-tap-tap.

One of them knocked on the screen door. It was a shallow rat-a-tat-tat, as if the visitor wanted his knock to go unheard.

"Come in, boys." Mr. Malarcher invited them in. "Good morning."

"Good morning." Their melancholy response reflected their moods. Spending the last few weeks of summer vacation working did not seem to make them particularly happy. They stood at the entrance of the house, not anxious to enter.

They nodded to Bobby and me. Then Emmett spotted the things spread out on the living room floor.

"Wow, look at all the baseballs!"

That broke the silence as Emmett hurried in to see everything. Jackie hung back, unsure of what to do. He just stood in the doorway, watching us.

Very slowly, so that it was almost unnoticeable, Mr. Malarcher moved to where Jackie was standing and escorted him into the living room.

"Here, boys, sit down. Artie, you and Bobby make room for Jackie and Emmett. I'll tell you how I got all of this."

The four of us sat on the floor amid baseballs and trophies and pictures, picking up and examining each item. Mr. Malarcher stood watching and smiling at us. Our questions started with how and where he had gotten everything. Mr. Malarcher settled into an old leather chair, his breath calm and easy, his eyes alive, dancing, and moving, as he began telling us stories.

For the next hour or so, Mr. Malarcher spun tales about baseball. His yarns of games played and places seen were alive in the telling. We could feel his joyous strength. We laughed with him as he told of impossible contests fought between men, playing the game they were created to play.

"I played against all the best ball players in America—Babe Ruth, Ty Cobb—all those players you fellas have probably read about. But, boys, there were some men that played baseball, and I'm telling you this, I believe that they were even better. I played with fellas like Cool Papa Bell, Satchel Paige, Double Duty Radcliffe, Bullet Rogan. They were really great ball players."

He hesitated, then said to the ghosts in his memory, "I love the dance of baseball."

His eyes seemed so far away; the entire time he spoke, he had a smile on his face. He'd sit back in his chair remembering, and then, he'd sit up quickly when he thought of a particular exciting game or play.

We sat there, little boys, quietly, listening to this wizened man tell stories of his youth.

"And then, there was the time in Alabama...."

Mr. Malarcher stopped, his eyes dropped. His body almost collapsed within itself. He became very still, as if frozen.

"Mr. Malarcher. Mr. Malarcher. You OK?" His dramatic change frightened me.

He was quiet for a second that felt like hours. He lifted his eyes that had become odd, unfocused. He spoke softly, almost a whisper.

"Fine. Yes, I'm fine."

The jubilance was gone. He had suddenly aged in front of us. The transformation was startling, like Lon Chaney Jr. when he changed into the wolfman in the movies. A quick and noticeable paleness crossed his brown skin as we sat on the floor quietly, watching.

Finally, "Well, boys, I've wasted enough of our time with my stories. Let's get to work."

But he didn't move.

"No. Come on, Mr. Malarcher. Your stories are real fun. Don't stop, please."

Jackie expressed how each of us felt. We didn't want the journey to end. This man had hooked us. He had been a near stranger who had become someone, someone whose property and well being had suddenly become important. He had made us feel valuable; that, in turn, made him imperative. This man who lived near us, here in the neighborhood, had done and seen things that were more exciting than anything we had ever imagined. He allowed us to travel with him through his memory. He told us stories in such a way that we were able to feel and see all the exotic cities and towns that he had visited. His eyes and smile had been alive with excitement and joy; he relived his young years and shared them with us.

We were just four little boys sitting in a semicircle on the floor in his tidy living room. Then, we were running the bases on ancient fields, riding the back roads of dusty towns, traveling all over the country and into foreign lands, chasing forgotten dreams.

Then, for some inexplicable reason, a cold chill grabbed the warmth from the room. It shivered the moment and froze it. The four of us sat on the floor at his feet quietly, not knowing what to do. We looked up at the man who had taken us with him, into his remembrances. He sat in the old chair, not moving, as the sun shined through the kitchen window behind him. The sunlight created a halo from the dust particles floating in the morning air as it caressed his darkened face. From a back room came the deep ticking sound of a lonely clock that taunted the awful silence.

"Mr. Malarcher? You OK? Mr. Malarcher?"

"Mr. Malarcher?"

Chapter five

Summer's End

"I'm OK. I'm OK. Honestly, boys, I am. I'm OK."

In his attempts to assure us, Mr. Malarcher succeeded only in continuing to alarm us.

Jackie leaned over and whispered to Emmett, "I'm getting scared, Bo."

"No, uh-uhh, I.... I think he's going to be OK...Uh-uhhh, Mr.. Mr. Malarcher, d.. d.. do.. you wa.. wa want some wa wa water? I'll get it for you."

"No, Emmett. I'm fine. Really. I'm sorry, boys; I didn't mean to frighten you. I promise you, I'm OK."

He inhaled very deeply; as he began to gather himself, color crept into and began to warm his face.

"Now, are you ready to get started? We have a great deal to do this morning."

He didn't move but sank even more deeply into his chair.

"Are you sure? Maybe I should get my mom." I was shaken by his sudden change.

"No, it's OK, Artie. I'm fine. I just thought about something that...." His voice trailed off into nothing. He stopped trying to talk and sat as if alone. Then very quietly, he spoke to us.

"Boys, I have told you quite a few stories about baseball and what it meant to me, what it meant to a lot of people. In many ways it was a wonderful and exciting time. I met so many incredible people. I got a chance to see so many places because of baseball. And because I was a manager, I got the chance to do so many things and to learn so much. Sometimes I think about what we had. You know, we owned all of our own teams, our own hotels, and restaurants. We had all the things we needed. I have a deep, deep fear…. I'm afraid that it is going to disappear. What I mean is this, what we had…have…well, it isn't perfect, but its ours…."

Again he hesitated and was silent. After a moment, he sat up and rubbed his chin, then looked at his hands, pondering his thoughts and how to express them. We sat mesmerized, not really understanding all that he was telling us, but somehow realizing it was important.

"A whole lot has happened that's changed the way things used to be. I suppose that's good, you know, that's progress. I just hope—I really hope—that as the bad things change, the good things don't change. I hope—but I'm not sure of this. I just hope we don't lose anything as we try to gain everything."

We sat at his feet looking up at him, unsure of how to respond, unsure of what he was going to say or do. The only thing that was certain was the sound that came from the unseen clock that stole the seconds from the late summer morning.

It is not often in a young person's life that particular moments become memorable ones, but somehow, in some way, I knew this was one. Mr. Malarcher seemed a very weary traveler, and we traveled with him.

The mood changed instantly, however, when he suddenly stood and scooped up one of the many baseballs that were spread out among the plaques and photos and trophies on the floor. He held the ball in his fingers for a second, then tossed it up about two feet with his left hand and quickly snatched it out of the air with his right. He then immediately dropped it into his left hand and tossed it up and again snatched it out of the air with his right. He repeated the private game of catch several times. The entire little exercise was done so quickly that it was hard to keep track of the ball. What was also amazing is that as he played his game of catch, he did it while deftly walking among the things that were haphazardly strewn on the floor and never stumbled on a thing.

It was as if he could see the floor out of one eye and watch the ball with the other. It was like those chameleons whose eyes turned all over the place when it was looking for flies and insects and stuff to eat that I had seen in the *National Geographic* magazine at school. I wondered if my dad could catch a ball like that, or even Mickey, or Jeff, or Pete.

Mr. Malarcher stopped his self-absorbed game of catch and sat down in the chair, still holding the ball. He was quiet a moment as he examined it. He must have recognized a name or something on the ball, for it forced a smile from his unwilling face. He sat back in the chair, his eyes closing briefly as his mood vanquished his smile.

After a moment he continued.

"I do know there are many things that happened that I have not told you. Because for now, you are just babies and are too young to understand or know about the bad part of life, about how tough life can be. I am not going to tell you about those things, but one day your parents will have to. They will teach you about the truth of what it means to be colored. Being colored in many parts of this country, well, it can be very, very hard. One day, you will have to understand how very hard it can be."

He paused, trying to find the right words. He sat back in the old leather chair, his eyes closed as he rubbed his brow. When he spoke next, it was very slowly and very softly.

"I will tell you this—baseball is beautiful, the most beautiful game in the world. Unfortunately, people play it."

He paused, then exhaled heavily.

"Sometimes people are not so beautiful. Sometimes people are very, very ugly."

That said, he abruptly stood up, stepped around us, and headed to the kitchen. The instant change in his disposition was remarkable. It was as if he had exorcised the demons in his memory with the angels of an optimistic and energetic present.

"Boys, what are you waiting for? Let's get to work."

We hustled to our feet and scrambled after him. We were like ducklings chasing after their mother. In just a short time, he had captured and intrigued us. We were fascinated by who he was, what he told us, and what went untold.

As he walked through his kitchen to the back door, he said over his shoulder, "Bobby, since you are the manager of our team, I will show you everything that has to be done. Then you take your team and show them what to do. Got it?"

"Mr. Malarcher, are you sure I can do this?"

This stopped him just as he was opening the door. He turned toward us, a bit exasperated. Bobby looked at him, his desperation apparent. It was clear Bobby was hoping he would not have to accept all this new and undesirable responsibility. His eyes flitted between the man in front of him and the boys who would probably not accept him as the manager. Jackie was already frowning at the prospect of Bobby being in charge.

"Bobby, you are the manager, and this is your team. If you believe that, so will they."

Bobby was momentarily silent and lost, doubting himself and the belief this man had in him. Yet, finally he seized the courage he had found in Mr. Malarcher's faith. He looked at us and said, "Come on, fellas. We got work to do." The words finally out of his mouth, he exhaled his fear. Then, with a nervous little smile crossing his lips, he turned to look up at his new mentor.

"Mr. Malarcher, what do you want us to do?"

"Let's go on outside and we'll talk about what has to be done."

We followed Mr. Malarcher out into the spacious yard behind his house. It encompassed a beautiful lawn and flowers next to it. The fence that guarded the front of the house also stretched around the perimeter of his land. In the front, the fence was about three feet high. On the side and back, the fence was five feet tall. Around the entire length of the fence were flowers of every imaginable color and hue with at least four or five blossoms in every group. There were about 100 groups, each separated by a few inches. Our job was to remove any weeds between each group of flowers.

In the middle of the yard were four trees planted like legs on a table. The trees were about the same height as the house. The branches hung down and were evenly trimmed so that you could walk under them without bending. Around the base of the four trees were more flowers; these were all behind white painted rocks. The dirt behind the rocks was six inches higher than the lawn. Between the four trees and behind the flowers was a birdbath that stood guard over the backyard. This was where we would spend the rest of our summer vacation.

"Mr. Malarcher, how do I know what I'm suppose to pull out and what I'm supposed to leave alone?"

"Well, Jackie, ask your manager." Jackie looked, not unkindly, at Bobby.

"Bobby, show Jackie which are plants I want to keep and which are weeds." Mr. Malarcher removed any doubt about who was in charge.

"Mr. Malarcher, I'm not real sure what to do." Bobby was looking real pitiful about then.

"OK, Bobby, come with me. You boys wait right there." He pointed to the wooden steps that led from his back porch into the yard. He then put his arm on Bobby's shoulder and led him to the fence. Bo, Jackie, and I sat down and watched, as Mr. Malarcher and Bobby talked to one another. We were unable to hear what they said, but every once in a while Mr. Malarcher knelt down, his young apprentice next to him, and they examined a plant. Some he'd toss into a pile, and others they would delicately touch and prop up. After a moment, they walked back to where we quietly sat. Mr. Malarcher sort of hung back and allowed Bobby to take the lead. Bobby looked at us a moment, then turned and looked up at Mr. Malarcher, who smiled at him and nodded his head. As he turned back to us, Bobby visibly exhaled, then said, "C'mon, Jackie. I'll show you which are the things we're suppose to pull out." Bobby spoke up for what may have been the first time in his life. He spoke with a courage he borrowed from Mr. Malarcher.

Jackie looked at Mr. Malarcher, then at Bobby. He was unwilling to confront Mr. Malarcher, yet he was also having trouble relinquishing his position to Bobby.

Mr. Malarcher had turned and stepped away to tend to his gardens, which obliged us to settle this on our own. The four of us walked across the yard and stood together in the shade of the four trees in the middle of the yard.

Bobby looked directly at Jackie and smiled. A bit hesitatingly he said, "Jackie, this is going to be fun. C'mon."

I stood next to Bobby, who was short for his age, not much taller than me. Jackie and Bo were standing next to each other facing us. Bo looked at Jackie, waiting for him to respond, but he said nothing. A long silence was interrupted only by the whistle of a lonely cardinal searching for his mate. Then, matter-of-factly, Bo made the decision. He altered the sides. Almost imperceptively, Bo edged closer to Bobby. Jackie noticed, we all did.

Mr. Malarcher had moved away from us and had gotten down on his knees to dig a hole with a small shovel near the fence on the other side of the yard. His concentration, however, was not on the hole, or the shovel in his hand, or the weeds in his garden. He was glancing ever so slightly at us, his head tilted awkwardly, so he could take in the little drama that was playing out in the green oasis that separated the grayness of the neighborhood from the lushness of the moment.

"Sure, yeah, you're right, Bobby." Jackie said. Then turning to Bo and me he said, "Let's get to work. C'mon, Artie. You, too, Bo. We got work to do."

With that, we were a team. Bobby was our manager, and Jackie wasn't.

That day and for the next two weeks, the four of us learned about baseball and planting flowers and separating the good from the bad.

Every morning we would gather in the back yard, pulling up weeds and planting bulbs. We would rake and water and weed the tidy lawn. We built small houses for birds we had rarely seen or even noticed. Every morning Bobby was the manager, and we were his team.

On rainy days we listened as Mr. Malarcher told stories about the people he met and the places he visited while playing baseball. Many of his stories, baseball related or not, had significance to life.

They were the *parables* according to Dave Malarcher. One of the memorable stories we heard was when Jackie was late. The three of us, Bobby, Bo (I was comfortable calling him that), and I, had been in the yard raking for about 30 minutes before Jackie arrived.

We heard him running before we saw him. He came down the alley and entered the yard through the back gate.

"Sorry I'm late. My cousins came over from the West Side, and we were talking for a long time, so I was real tired this morning. What are we doing today?"

"I see. So you were tired this morning cause you were busy last night, huh? Is that it? That's your story?" Mr. Malarcher seemed upset.

"Yes, sir. My auntie doesn't have a car, so they, my cousins and her, came on the streetcar. My ma said it was OK."

"She did, did she? Well, I'm not happy about it, and it isn't OK with me, and I'll tell you why. This team is depending on you. If a member of the team isn't around to do the work, then the entire team struggles. So what happens is the team is forced to eliminate the member that isn't helping. Do you understand what I'm saying, Jackie?"

"I guess so."

"You guess so? Uh. I see. You guess so. Well, let me tell you a story to illustrate, and then maybe you will know.

"A farmer had a mule and an ox. Every morning the mule and the ox would go out to the fields and pull the plow for the farmer. It was hard work, and each night, after they had completed the hard day's work, they would trudge back to the barn and rest up for the next morning's work. Well, don't you know that one morning the ox decided that he really didn't feel like getting up that early, so he told the mule that he was just too tired to help, and he stayed in his stall all day. The mule, however, decided to go to the fields and help the farmer with the work. Late that evening, when the mule got back to the barn, the ox asked him if the farmer had said anything about his absence. The mule told the ox that the farmer hadn't said a word. So the ox relaxed for the night. He felt just as relaxed the next morning and decided not to get up and help the farmer then, either. But the ole, trusty mule did as he had always done; he got up and went to the fields to help the farmer.

"That night when the mule came back to the barn, the ox again asked him if the farmer had said anything about him not showing up. The mule told him that the farmer had not said a word but had gone to town that evening after the plowing was done. That next morning the ox got up extra early so he wouldn't be late to the fields. When he saw the farmer, the ox told him that he was certainly ready to get to work that good and bright morning. The farmer responded that he really didn't need him that morning and the ox might as well go on back to the barn. But the ox protested, saying that he was certainly ready to get to work. The farmer shook his head and told him he could work that day if he wanted, but he had made an appointment for him with the butcher that night.

"You see, boys, we all make choices, and sometimes we make good choices and sometimes we make bad choices. It is always important to try to make good choices."

On another morning, Bobby was late, and Mr. Malarcher did not accept his reason for being late at all.

"Bobby, you're the manager, so it is even more important that you be here on time. Your team expects you to show them the way by setting a good example. But, there is another reason for you to be on time, and that is because of our agreement.

"Now, our agreement was for you to pay me only a part of the money you've saved. I have decided that I am not going to take that money, even though it is rightly mine. I've decided that because you have done a good job as manager—up to now, anyway. What I think I am going to do is let you keep it, but only if you promise me you will never be late again. What do you think?"

"Wow! Thank you, Mr. Malarcher, for letting me keep the money, but I really tried to get here on time. I have to get up real early to do my paper route. That's why I was late."

"Bobby, I know you have a paper route, but you also have responsibilities here. In order to complete everything that you are responsible for, you are going to have to be a good planner and not let anything mess them up. Sometimes that means you may have to get up early in the morning, or go to bed early at night. You can't make up excuses for yourself, because people won't listen to them. You have to understand that people don't care about what you say—they only care about what you do."

He was looking at Bobby but was speaking to all four of us.

"There are a thousand excuses for poor behavior and failure, but only one reason for success."

"And what is that, the one reason for success?" Bobby had gotten bold in his managerial role.

Mr. Malarcher smiled at his protégé but didn't say a word, which was a curious habit he had that we learned to endure. We waited as he went through the ritual. It would start when we asked a question that would give him a chance to teach us some great thing through one of his parables. He would look up and shake his head slowly as if to say, "Lord, what am I to do with these boys of yours?"

Then he'd be quiet, letting the silence speak for him. After a moment he would start by looking at his hands and silently moving his lips as if speaking to them. He would hold up one hand first, peering at the back of it, and then very curiously, he would inspect his palm, as if it were the first time he had ever seen it. He would wait again, and his words would be preceded by a smile that would creep slowly from his eyes to his cheeks and then his mouth. He would drop the hand that had been so thoroughly inspected to his side. Then, very softly, as if an afterthought, he'd speak. This is exactly what he did when he answered Bobby's question:

"When you refuse to make excuses and begin to accept responsibility for the things you do, that is when you will be on the road to success. Remember this. It is while you're on the road itself that you will be at your very best."

Mr. Malarcher in many ways enjoyed our company. I didn't know whether he had any children or not, but for the two weeks we spent working in his yard, he treated us as if we were his own sons, and the time went quickly.

It was near the beginning of school and the work at Mr. Malarcher's house was ending. I sat at the breakfast table and ate the cereal my mother had made for me.

"Artie, I want you to know that we are proud of you and how you have gotten up every morning and gone over to Mr. Malarcher's house all by yourself. He called and told us that you have been doing a really good job."

"Thanks, Mom. It's been real fun. Bobby n' Jackie n' Bo have been real fun, too."

"Good. I'm happy that you have enjoyed working hard. That's always good. Remember to always do that—to always work hard at everything you do, OK, honey? Maybe one of these days, when you are a little bigger, you will be able go to work with your dad on the milk truck like your brother Pete."

"Yea, when I'm big like Pete, I can go to work with Dad, too."

Pete worked with our father on Saturday mornings during the summer. It was a good experience for him, plus Dad paid him a dollar for the day. I eagerly anticipated the day that I would be old enough to go with Dad on the milk route.

School was opening soon, and like most kids, I was sorry to see the summer come to an end. The last day we were to tend to the lawn and gardens at Mr. Malarcher's house was like all the other days. We worked quietly under the management of our boss Bobby, who had become confident in his role. We were just putting away the garden tools when we heard, "Waaaaterrmeeeeloooosss, waaaaterrmeeee-loooosss, come and get yo' waaaaterrmeeeeloooosss."

It was one of the many peddlers who sold their wares in the neighborhood. They informed everyone of their presence with a song. Any day during the spring, summer, or fall, they rode up and down the alleys singing their melodic tunes. Watermelon Man, Ragman, Junk Man, you could hear their songs ringing through the streets. The kids would come running, games temporarily halted, just to see the wagons and the horses that pulled them. The alley would smell of the pungent odor of horse droppings, a lingering reminder of the peddler's faithful visits.

The Watermelon Man peddled juicy Mississippi watermelons up and down the alleys of our neighborhood. We waited for him to pass. The wagons were usually filled with straw with huge watermelons lying in it like green eggs in a giant bird's nest.

Mr. Malarcher, to our surprise, was almost as excited as we were to see the horse-drawn wagon. He had, however, gotten a shovel and a paper bag and was opening his back gate.

"Boys, I have to beat Mrs. Lee to the prize."

We had no idea what he was talking about. We just watched with anticipation as the hawker of melons crooned his selling song.

"Waaaaterrmeeeeloooosss. Come and get yo' waaaaterrmeeee-loooosss."

The horse clomped slowly down the alley, his hoofs hitting the pavement in rhythm with his master's song.

"Waaaaterrmeeeelooooosss." Clomp, clomp. "Come and get yo' waaaaterrmeeeelooooosss."

When he saw us at the back gate, he pulled the reins he held between his fingers, "Whoa there, Buttons. Come on now. Whoa, boy. All right. Dere ya go."

The horse grunted in protest and then stopped in front of us. The man on the wagon reached next to his leg and pulled on a wooden handle that was as thick as a broomstick; the wooden stick was attached to the side of the wagon. This action pushed a padded block against the front wheel. The wheel was about four feet tall and had wooden spokes. Around the circumference of the wheel was a metal band. When the block pressed against the wheel, it acted as a brake.

With the wagon now secure, the old man looked down at us with runny eyes, a smile on his rugged face. He hadn't shaved in a few days, so you could see the gray stubble that was winning the battle of dominance with the black hair on his dark brown chin.

"Can I get'cha one of these juicy Mississippi watermelons, sah? They's as fresh as dis mornin's butterfly. Whatcha say?"

This was said with great emphasis, assuring the purchaser that these were quality watermelons. Mississippi-fresh watermelons.

He deftly jumped to the ground with remarkable agility and grace. He landed as lightly as a baby's kiss.

"Just got dese here from Missisip' dis mornin'. They's as fresh as a pastor's breath on a Sunday morning. Dat is fo sho'!"

I had noticed that even the manner of his speech was melodic. His thick southern accent was deep and filled with a mournful joy.

Mr. Malarcher had a broad smile on his face and spoke to the man with a comfort that spoke of mutual respect and understanding.

"I hadn't planned on getting a watermelon today, but I guess these young men would like to have one. Is that a good idea, fellas? Would you like one?"

"Oh yeah! Heck, yea! Uh huh!" we chorused in unison, like hungry baby birds.

"Well, OK, my friend. We'll get one. Just came in from Mississippi, you say?"

"Yep, sho' did. Just got in dis mornin'."

"Well, I guess something good should come up from ole Missisip, if you know what I mean."

"Yea, well, I guess you gotta know how to get along down dere, that's fo' sho'."

"Yes, that is for sure. Let's see what you have in that wagon of yours."

"I got the most sweetest, the most juiciest, the most bestest letters from home you ever done seen. Yessah das fo' sho'."

As he walked to the back of his wagon, we got a little closer to the horse. It was dark brown and enormous. We laughed as the horse let loose with a huge discharge that fell to the ground like old potatoes. He must have eaten a huge breakfast because he deposited what looked like enough to fill several bushel baskets right in the middle of the alley.

Jackie was the first to respond.

"Yeow, I never seen so much poop in my life!"

He was right and we laughed and laughed, pointing at the mess in the middle of the alley. That is, we laughed until Mr. Malarcher gave us a disapproving glance. We then quieted down.

When the Watermelon Man had finished his sale, he leaped back onto the wagon as quickly and easily as he had gotten off.

"Well, sah, ah preciate da bisness. Ah'll see ya nex tom. Bless ya'll now. OK, c'mon now, Buttons, getchup."

He released the brake with a kick from his right foot, then made clicking sounds with his mouth and snapped the reins lightly on the horse's rump. The old horse strained hard against the stagnant weight of the wagon before the wheels gave up and the wagon began to lurch forward.

"Attaboy. Dere ya go. Alright dere. OK, bye now, boys. I gotta go. Getcha up now. Attaah boy. Getcha up now. Attaah boy. Heeyaaah. See ya later, boys."

We watched as the horse and wagon creaked down the alley. The load of watermelons rocked back and forth in the bed of straw in time with the slow role of the horse's gait. The Mississippi peddler continued his late summer call.

"Waaaaterrrrrmeeeellloooos. Come n' get'cho waaaaterrrrr-meeeellloooos!!"

Like an early morning shower, his song faded into the long summer afternoon.

"Waaaaterrrrrmeeeellloooosss. Getcho waaaaterrmeee........"

Mr. Malarcher lugged the great big, juicy melon into the kitchen. We gathered around him anxiously as he sliced it into generous portions, giving each of us a piece that was much larger than we could have possibly eaten. Until that moment, I had never liked watermelon very much. But for that single instant, on that late summer day, sitting on the back steps of Mr. Malarcher's house with a team of boys who had found something wonderful, and with the smell of freshly mown grass all around us, I don't think I ever tasted anything quite so sweet.

"Boy, this is the best watermelon I have ever had." Bo was ecstatic. There were grunts of our affirmation. "Uh huh, sure is sweet and juicy!"

We continued slurping, grunting, and smacking our lips as we consumed the juicy red fruit, our mouths dripping with its sweetness.

"Did you hear him call them a 'letter from home'? That's a nickname for watermelons, 'a letter from home.' That Watermelon Man said these were from Mississippi. That's where my mama's family lives."

"My mom's from Baton Rouge, Louisiana." I didn't know exactly where Baton Rouge was, but Mom had told us that was where she was from.

"I'm from Louisiana, too." It was Mr. Malarcher. He set a paper bag at his feet. I had noticed while we were eating the delicious watermelon, he was in the alley scooping up something, and whatever he had found was in that bag.

"I went to college in New Orleans, Louisiana. That's when I decided I could be a good baseball player."

"Mr. Malarcher, what's that in the bag?" I was curious because he placed the paper bag rather gently on the ground next to him, a sly smile on his mouth.

"You want to know what's in the bag, do ya? This bag has you more curious than Louisiana and college and anything else. Is that right, Artie?"

"Yes, sir, it does."

"OK, boys, what I have here is what is called fertilizer. It is what Mrs. Lee and I battle over."

We looked into the bag and reacted as a bunch of little boys would. We laughed and laughed and fainted in mock disgust, rolling around in the grass in reaction to the paper bag filled with steamy horse droppings.

"Mr. Malarcher, that's horse dodo. What are you doing with that? You shoulda let Mrs. Lee have it."

Mr. Malarcher laughed deeply at our antics. His laugh and smile came easy, easier than when we first met him. He looked at us with a kind yet mischievous twinkle in his eye.

"Mrs. Lee has a stunning backyard, and that's because of what she and I know about growing beautiful gardens. The best part is that what we need is free, free for the taking. All people who want nice flowers have to do is to open their eyes and see, to take advantage of what's right there in front of them.

"Boys, in the alley, it was horse dodo. When I put it into the bag, it became manure, and when I brought it into my yard, it became fertilizer."

This was all said with a magnificent flourish. His arms and hands were thrusting and evocative, putting on a demonstration for us, pointing dramatically at each declaration.

"It may seem strange to you, but everything in your life has value. It all depends on how well you use it."

We sat looking up at him, truly not understanding what he was saying to us.

With a juicy laugh between gulps of melon, Bo said, "But, Mr. Malarcher, that's still just stinky old horse dodo."

Mr. Malarcher's smile faded for a split second before he recovered it. He looked at his hands, examining them—first his palms, and then he turned them over and contemplated the back of them. He spoke before he raised his head, and then he looked directly at Bo.

"Emmett, I think you will find that there are many things in life that have great value and great importance, even when they appear grotesque or disgusting."

Chapter six

Schooled

"It's time to get up,
so hurry, hurry up,
my little buttercup."

"Maaaa, stop singing that song!"

I heard Pete's protesting plea come from beneath the covers. Mom often awakened us by singing what we referred to as the "get up" song. We hated it. Mom was trying to be nice when she woke us up for school, but we still hated that song.

"Boys, come on now. You don't want to be late for your first day back to school."

Mom was in the kitchen making breakfast for us as Carol was walking out of the back door. She had to be at school earlier than we, so she left for school just as my brothers and I were getting up. This was an anxious day for her because she was trying out for the cheerleaders at Englewood High School. Last night she had told us how excited she was. As a sophomore she was overjoyed to have a chance to be on the squad.

"Mom, I really think I have a good chance to make the cheerleading squad. I'm so nervous, though. I hope I don't mess up. Sharon said she thinks I have a good chance, too. Do you think I'm going to do OK?"

"I'm sure you will. Just give it your best, OK, sweetheart? If you do make it, we'll celebrate, and if you don't, we'll celebrate anyway because we know you've done your best. You be careful on your way to school, and we'll see you this evening."

"All right, bye now. See ya later, boys. Hey, Marty, good luck in first grade. I know you'll do well in Mrs. Smith's class. Pete, Art, you boys have a great day, too."

Our chorus of "byes" and "see yas" followed her out of the door. We could hear her as she called out to our cousins on the second floor.

"Good morning, Aunt Monie. Please tell Mick, Jeff, and Billy to have a great day."

"I will, and good luck, Carol. I hope you make the cheerleading squad."

"Thanks, Auntie. Bye...."

I couldn't understand the rest of what she said as she ran down the stairs on her way to school. All the kids in the building were excited that Carol was trying out to be a cheerleader at Englewood. Her best friend, Sharon Hayes, lived in the building next to ours, and Carol would stop by her apartment so they could go to school together. The two of them were the oldest kids in the neighborhood, so our social understandings regarding clothes, music, and slang filtered down from them. Consequently, it seemed perfectly reasonable that being a cheerleader was the best thing a person could be.

Carol was our protector. She was taller, and tougher, than any of the other kids in the neighborhood. My brothers and I firmly believed that all cheerleaders were tall and strong and tough.

"OK, boys, better get going. You've got to get up, now."

We were slowly beginning to sit up in bed. Marty and Pete were moving faster than I was.

"Marty, honey, today is your first day at school for the whole day. You're now in first grade. Aren't you excited? No more kindergarteners in the Miller house. No, sir, all of the young Miller men are in school all day. I know I'm excited about that."

Mom was stretching with both hands on her back as she looked out the kitchen window. Her last words were said with joyous melancholy.

"Yea, Mom. Pete and Artie, Jeff and Billy, and I are all gonna walk to and from school together."

Marty was overjoyed; this would be the first time that he would attend school for a full day. Kindergarten for public school students was for only a half a day. The first half of the year, each child attended school only in the afternoon, and the second half of the school year, the students attended class only in the morning.

"Pete, Artie, you make sure and watch out for your brother now, you hear?"

"Oh, yeah, Mom, of course we're gonna watch out for little ole liver-lips here."

Pete was pushing Marty toward the bathroom.

"First thing I'm gonna do is make sure that those naps on top of his head get brushed. They're about to pull his brains out."

"Uh-uhhh. You're not touching my head. Maaaa, tell Pete to leave me alone!"

"Pete, leave your brother alone. He can brush his hair himself. Artie, you get moving, too. No one is going to be late. You guys have to hurry up so you can eat breakfast before you go to school.

The sweet smell of our morning meal drifted through the house. I could hear Mom from the kitchen as I lingered in bed for just a moment more. The wonderful sound of bacon sizzling in the frying pan teased the morning sounds.

"Artie, you boys are going to stop downstairs at your cousins before you go, right?"

"Yep. We're all going to walk together for the first time." At this point I was sitting on the side of the bed as I watched my mother cooking breakfast for us. The summer had ended nicely. I had learned so much from Mr. Malarcher and liked working with Jackie and Bobby and Bo a lot because they were older than I was, but also because I felt that they treated me like I was not a little kid. Much of that had to do with Mr. Malarcher.

I was excited about all of us going to school. I didn't mention it to my brothers or cousins, but I was hoping that Frances, the cute girl on the first floor, was also going to walk with us.

This would be the first time I would see her since I had run away from her the morning I had to go to Mr. Malarcher's house. Fortunately, I had been successful in avoiding her.

"You go get washed up, and tell your brothers to hurry up." Mom instructed.

"Hey, Mom, we're all going to be in school for the whole day." I wanted to emphasize the point.

"Yes, that's exciting for all of us, believe me."

For some reason, she shook her head from side to side when she said this. Mom was often mysterious in her ways. After a moment, she yelled to us, "Hey, you guys! I folded your clothes and put them in the front room on the ironing board. Get dressed before you come in here to eat. Got it?"

"Yep, we got it." "You betcha." "Yep, we're coming."

"Hey, we're getting pancakes this morning! I'm going fast as Jesse Owens, Mom, just watch me."

I bounded up from the bed and past my brothers who were just emerging from the bathroom. Pete was squeezing Marty's head in his hands, muttering in a strange Slavic- accented voice.

"I'll squeeze your head into a pin ball."

Our father had threatened us with this when the three of us wrestled with him. He would grab one of us while the brothers he hadn't caught jumped on his back. In a mock wrestlers hold he would shout, "I vill squeedze yo hade inna peen ball." He then would follow that up with a hysterical laugh. "HA HA HA HA HAAAAAA."

At that point we would abandon the captured brother to the grip of our father.

Pete was making a great impersonation of Dad, and Marty shrieked in feigned terror as he got away from him and ran to the protection of our mother.

"Mom, Mom, save me, save me."

Marty was giggling the entire time as he wedged himself between the kitchen sink and Mom, so he could escape his tormenting brother, who happened to be equally as giddy.

"I'm gonna squeedse that hade!" Pete howled as he lurched stiff-legged after his youngest brother. A part of the act was to take on the image of Frankenstein's monster to increase the element of dread. Pete also added the obligatory out-stretched arms and held his head back. It was all a wonderful imitation of a miniature Bela Lagosi.

"No you not, no you not!" Marty shrieked again as he ducked behind Mom.

"Boys, stop. Stop. Stop it now! Calm down, you hear me! Now sit down and eat. C'mon, boys, stop it. Now, did you guys do a good job washing up? I mean, did you use soap and did you wash behind your necks and ears?"

"Maa, of course we did. Didn't we, Mart?" Pete said in mock disbelief. How could Mom ever think that her precious sons would ever wash up without doing it thoroughly?

"Uh huhh. We sure did, soap and everything."

Marty's muffled response came filtered through his pancake-and-maple-syrup-filled mouth. He wasn't about to miss the delicious breakfast Mom had cooked and had quickly begun eating when Pete stopped his teasing.

"Marty, did you say the blessing before you began eating?"

"Uh.... I think so...."

"Marty, the truth now. Pete, you wait, too."

"Now I lay me down to sleep, I pray..."

"Not that one, liver-lips." Pete was laughing at Marty's efforts. "You're not going to bed. That one is for nighttime. Remember this one? "Thank you Lord for these gifts we're about to receive from your bounty through Christ our Lord. Amen.'"

"Thank you, Pete, but remember we also say; 'in the name of the Father and the Son and the Holy Spirit. Amen.' Then you cross yourself like this." She then touched her forehead, her stomach, and her left and right shoulders while repeating "The Father, the son, and the Holy Spirit."

We were devout Catholics, and the Church and Christ were important parts of our family.

"Artie, you better hurry before your brothers eat everything. But you make sure you wash up real well, and don't forget to use soap. Remember, you have to be nice and clean for your first day, OK?"

"OK, Ma!" The aroma of bacon and pancakes filled the bright morning as I quickly washed up using soap as Mom had asked.

"You guys save some for me!" I yelled as I sprinted out of the bathroom, scrambled over the bed in the dining room, and streaked into the kitchen.

"Whoa, slow down there, Artie. I've made plenty of pancakes."

"I know, Ma, thanks, but you'all better not eat everything up!" I demanded.

My brothers smiled at me with open mouths.

"I wouldn't let you go to school without eating, Artie." Mom, always the peacemaker, had the unenviable and impossible task of trying to stop my brothers and me from teasing one another.

We ate hurriedly, knowing that our cousins and friends were waiting. This was the first day of school, and we were as excited as every other youngster and parent in the neighborhood.

"Hey, you guys ready? It's time to go." Pete was ready. "I'm going downstairs to see if Mick n' em are ready."

"We're comin'. Wait up. Come on, Marty. Pete's leaving. We gotta go." I yelled for Marty to hurry up. He had to go to the bathroom after breakfast.

"I'm coming," Marty yelled as he came running out of the bathroom with his pants still undone.

"Marty, fix your pants! Mom, we're going. See you later! Bye, Mom. Bye!" Pete hollered.

"See you later, boys. I love you. Be careful and work hard. Make sure Marty gets to his classroom, Pete. I'm counting on you, you, too, Artie. Marty, you do well today. I'll be waiting to hear how your day went."

I held open the screen door as Marty came flying out with a huge grin that lit up his face. I could barely keep up with him as he ran down the back stairs, jumping and skipping over as many of them as he could without falling down. When we reached the second floor, Pete and our cousins were standing together looking up and smiling, waiting for us. I stood and watched as they patted Marty on the back. They encircled him. Mickey was in eight A and would be graduating in January. Pete and Jeff in seven B, Billy was in two A, Marty was in one B, and I was in four B. Together, the six of us started for school.

"Well, fellas, looks like the Green and Miller boys are about to take over McCosh school." Cousin Mickey was pleased that all of us would be in school together.

Their last name was Green, and often we had to correct people who had mistaken all of us for brothers. It wasn't infrequent that one of us would hear, "Hey, which are you, a Green or a Miller?"

This happened regularly during the first month or two, when teachers had one of us in their class the previous semester.

Our cousin's mother was at the back door. Aunt Ramona, my mom's sister and a surrogate parent to my siblings and me, wished us all a great beginning of the school year.

"You boys do well in school, make us proud. Look out for Marty and Billy. Be careful. I want to hear how school went when I get home from work tonight. Be good, and work hard boys."

A chorus of "Good bye, Aunt Monee's," "See yaw's," "Bye, Mom," was lost amid the sound of our pounding feet as the six of us scurried down the back stairs. We all raced to the bottom of the steps, laughing as we started to school.

In the back yard, Frances and her older sister Beverly were jumping rope. They stopped as we cascaded down the last steps that led to the yard. Looking at the group of us boys, they moved closer to one another and whispered, then with hands over their mouths, they giggled. They were both quite pretty with hair that fell down to their shoulders in soft curls, bangs lightly brushing against their foreheads. Tiny yellow bows that matched their skirts were placed neatly in their hair. They were standing with one hand on their hips, the other covering their mouths, their heads close. They looked at us, then at each other, then shook their heads like disapproving mothers waiting for their wayward children.

"Hey, Artie, there's Frances." Pete was grinning from ear to ear. All the fellas were looking at me.

"I don't care. Heck, I don't even like her." I was too embarrassed to say anything else. But I didn't say it loud enough for her to hear me.

Out of the corner of my eye, I stole a glance in her direction. She smiled and hid a little wave. I waved back wiggling my fingers in her direction, hoping she would be the only one to see my gesture. I was fortunate, no one saw it. With the morning formalities over, we began our trek to school.

Beverly and Frances had stopped to pick up one of their friends and lingered behind us. I forgot about Frances and listened to my cousins and brothers as they talked.

We walked together through the alley up to 64th Street and over to Champlain Ave. The walk and the neighborhood were familiar. Every telephone pole and streetlight carried a memory; they were used in our games as goal for hide and seek or tag. We knew every crack in the sidewalks on our walk to McCosh Elementary School. All along the way we greeted kids we hadn't seen for the summer. The bright, late summer morning greeted us with warmth.

"Hey, fellas." It was Jackie. "You all ready for school?"

"Yea, about as ready as you can get." Mickey spoke for all of us. "How did you like working at Mr. Malarcher's?"

"It was all right. He had all kind of baseball stuff and talked a lot about the old days. Yea, he was a cool cat for an old man."

To us, Jackie had given Mr. Malarcher the ultimate compliment; he was a "cool cat." I thought so as well. I hadn't gone by to see him as he had suggested, but I waved at him the day before school started. I had seen him in his backyard gardening. He had a wide-brimmed straw hat on his head and was bent over his beloved flowers, putting horse fertilizer on them. When he leaned back to stretch his back, his closed eyes, opened them, and spotted me. He nodded, and with a slight smile, he waved back at me. He truly was a cool cat.

"Hey, fellas." It was Bo. "YY yawl' ready for school?"

"Hi, man. I'm as ready as can be. Whose class you in?" Jeff asked.

"Ole lady C-C-C-Campbell." Bo shook his head in disappointment. Mrs. Campbell was known as a very strict teacher, and Bo had difficulty in school. He had repeated a grade a year or so earlier and was older than most of the kids in the class. Evidently, this was going to be another rough year for him.

"Hey, Bo, things will be OK. I hear Mrs. Campbell is not that mean."

"Thanks, Pete. I hope yo..you're right."

He and Pete were in Mrs. Campbell's class together. Pete was going into the seventh grade, which was considered the upper grades. Because he had skipped fourth grade, he was going to be younger than the other kids in his class. He was able to do fourth-grade work as a third grader, so he had, with our parent's urging, gone from third grade directly to fifth grade. Academically, it was a great decision. He had done remarkably well and enjoyed the more challenging work, particularly the math. He had taught me and a few of the kids in our apartment building the multiplication times tables when we were in the first grade, which gave all of us an advantage. It also meant that Pete was really looked up to by the kids in the building. Being smart, we all knew, was important. All of our parents had pounded it into our heads that if we were going to be a credit to our race, then we would be required to always do our best at school.

At the time, I don't really believe I understood this "credit to our race" thing and what it really meant, but since every adult I knew kept insisting on us doing well in school and being a credit to our race, most of us accepted that idea as fact.

The social adjustment for Pete had been a little more difficult. The girls in his class thought he was a nice boy. Any "school-boy" crushes Pete might have entertained fell on girls who thought he was too young for him.

At recess, he wasn't able to keep up with the bigger boys in some of their games. In gym class he often felt the embarrassing sting of being picked last when the class was separated into two teams. Fortunately, our cousin Jeffrey who was also in Pete's class would pick him early if he were selected as captain of a team.

As we came closer to the school, the low hum of children's eager voices drifted to us. It was impossible to distinguish a particular voice or word, but the morning air was filled with a light-hearted gaiety. When we turned down Champlain where the school building was located, a kaleidoscope of colors invaded our senses. Hundreds of children in bright colors danced and bounced in front of the school. The screeching noise of happy children ricocheted off the school building. Standing guard at either end of the street were wooden horses painted a bright yellow with the words "school crossing" printed in black across the top, making the street open and safe for games of catch, jump rope, tag, and laughter.

The teachers were outside among the kids. You could see them as they loomed over everyone. Mr. Yamada, the gym teacher, had a boy by the back of his collar already, and it was just the first day of school. Undoubtedly, the wayward boy would get a ruler across the palm of his hand for some infraction. Mr. Yamada was fair, but strict. If he caught you messing up, the punishment you received was legendary.

When we got to school, the boys and girls lined up at different entrances. We all lined up in order of class, with the first-graders in front. We all stood with Marty to make sure he felt comfortable. We knew no one would pick on him, or bully him, because he was always nice and shared things with other kids. Moreover, he had older brothers and cousins around.

McCosh School was an enormous three-story brick building with the playground situated in the back. It took up nearly an entire city block and had approximately 700 students.

My class was on the second floor of the old building, and my teacher, Mrs. Seahigh, was grouchy and old, much like the building. I didn't like her because she seemed unduly cruel to my friends and she had horrible halitosis. The rumor in school was that she had bad breath because she ate her own socks for breakfast.

As I walked into my classroom, I saw the familiar faces of friends I hadn't seen since the end of school in June. We greeted one another, getting reacquainted. We had all gone to school together since kindergarten.

"Hi, Artie." It was Freddy Moore, my best friend at school. We generally didn't see one another during the summer because his apartment was a few blocks from where I lived. He was a little shorter than I and was a real friendly kid.

"Hi, Freddy." Just then Mrs. Seahigh entered the room, announced by the heavy sound of her shoes. She looked at us with a scowl.

I was now in fourth grade, and even though I had always been a very good student, Mrs. Seahigh made me nervous; I realized that fourth grade was not going to be easy. This was the grade that Pete had skipped. I wasn't quite as smart as he, so I wasn't allowed to skip it and go directly to fifth grade. I watched Mrs. Seahigh and her big, black, old-lady shoes as she came clomping into the classroom. I suddenly wished I had gone straight to fifth grade.

"Find a seat and sit in it. I will assign you permanent seats later. Be quiet while I check my roster."

That was it. No "Good morning. Hello. Welcome. How was your summer?" Nothing, nothing, but sit down and shut up. School had started, and summer vacation was abruptly over.

I stood and stared for a moment like a deer stuck in the lights of an on-coming car, unable to move, as my friends scrambled to find seats. When I came to my senses, all the kids had found places as far from her desk as possible. The only one of the 33 in the room that was still empty was right in front of her huge oak desk. I stood motionless, searching desperately for another empty place. I searched in vain.

"Well, young man, there is only one seat left. Are you going to move your feet or not?"

She stood there, her dreadful foot tapping on the floor, tap-tap-tap-tap-tap, as she waited for me to make my way to the empty desk.

Some of the kids giggled as I reluctantly and painfully moved through the rows of wooden desks to that ominous empty one. Mrs. Seahigh glared at me as I gradually made it to the most terrible spot in the classroom. I felt terrible, and this was just the first day of school.

Fortunately, I only had to sit there for a few days. Our permanent seats were assigned alphabetically so I sat in front of my friend Freddy

Moore. He was a good student also, and sometimes we teamed up on homework assignments. We had really done a good job on one about dinosaurs that helped form our close friendship.

After lunch on that first day of school, Mrs. Seahigh gave us the outline of what she expected of us. We were given books that we were expected to keep at school in our desks. The top of the desks opened and that's where we kept our books, papers, and pencils. Mrs. Seahigh also informed us that she would have weekly inspections of our desks, so we had better keep them neat.

When the dismissal bell rang, we all jumped from our seats and lined up at the door. It was going to be a long year. Mrs. Seahigh rose from her desk and opened the door to the hallway. When we walked out of the class, we joined all the other students in our wing of the building. All the teachers had their classes in the hallway, and we all lined up as the teachers led us down the stairs, where we joined the rest of the children heading home from school. I saw Pete and Jeff escorting Marty and Billy on Champlain Ave. They looked over the crowd of kids, searching for me. I waved several times before they spotted me and waved back.

"Hey, fellas."

"Hey, Artie, how was Mrs. Seahigh?" Pete knew of her reputation.

"She was mean and stuff."

We began walking home together. Mickey wasn't there because he was a patrol boy. Pete and Jeff were too, but they didn't have to start until next week. Because they had younger brothers, they were allowed to walk them home to make certain they got home safely for the first week of school. We turned toward home, talking together about school and friends and what some of them said they had done during the summer.

We had gotten to Eberhardt Ave., the street just before ours, when Freddy Moore came flying toward us with a strange look on his face. Jeff stopped him.

"Hey, man, you all right?"

Freddy sighed. He looked frightened. He bent over, trying to catch his breath. As he gasped for air, he took furtive glances behind him; he was running from some one or some thing. He stood next to Jeff, who was much taller. He kept moving and crouching down as if he were hiding, using Jeff as a shield

"There… was…a … man… that... scared me!!" Freddy was close to hysteria.

"What man? I don't see anyone. What happened? How did he scare you? What did he do?"

"He wanted me to come with him…. Ah …I…."

"What are you talking about? Come with him? Where?" The entire time he was questioning Freddy, Jeff's head spun like it was on a swivel, his eyes wide as he looked, searching in every direction for the mysterious man who had frightened Freddy so terribly.

Again Freddy began, his words coming sporadically between deep gulps of air. His eyes were darting everywhere. He stood closer to Jeff than he would have normally, using the bigger boy as a shield, so he could hide from whatever had come after him.

"It was a man…he...wan….ahh jeezz."

"What are you talkin' about? Who?" Everyone was gathered around Freddy. He was our friend and someone, someone, a man, had frightened him. But, we didn't understand why he was so scared. Did the man want to beat him up? If so, why?

Once again he tried to explain what had happened.

"It was some man. Ahhhh" As Freddy tried to tell us what had happened to him, he could no longer hold it together. He began to shake, his shoulders slumped over, and he cried. He bellowed a deep, fearful cry, almost screaming, as long jagged sobs rose from the deepest part of his being.

We all gathered around him, patting him on his back. Confused and frightened, none of us were sure of what to do. It was clear, however, something was terribly wrong. It was also clear that we were all very, very frightened.

"We better get somebody." Pete was thinking clearly.

"Yea, we better get Mom or Dad." I remembered my lessons from that summer.

"Freddy. Freddy, your mama or daddy at home?" Jeffrey had leaned over, talking right into Freddy's eyes.

After a moment, his heaving sobs subsided and Freddy spoke, slowly.

"Nooo. Noooo. Ain't nobody home. They're at work."

"My pop's home. C'mon. We gotta get goin'," Jeff said as he continued looking for the strange man who had come after Freddy.

"Let's go." Nothing else needed to be said . The five of us circled Freddy and we ran as fast as the slowest kid (Billy) could run.

We got to our building and tore up the back stairs. Then Freddy started crying again. We began screaming for Uncle Jimmy, Jeff's and Billy's dad.

"Dad!" "Uncle Jimmy!" "Dad!" "Uncle Jimmy!" " Daaaaaad!"

We all scrambled through the screen door into the apartment. Thank goodness the back door was open, or we would have all piled into one another trying to get into the apartment. Uncle Jimmy came running in from the front room where he had been working on some of his drawings, because he had a pencil behind one of his ears and reading glasses on the end of his nose.

"What's the commotion all about? What happened? Who's that boy?"

"Daddy, there was this man and...." "Yea, and he scared...." "Some stranger...."

We were all trying to talk at once as Freddy continued wailing.

"Stop it! Now one at a time. Jeffrey, what is going on?"

"We were walking home from school when Freddy...this is Freddy Moore, he lives over on Eberhardt. He's in Artie's class."

"Uh huh." I nodded my head in agreement.

"OK, but what happened?" Uncle Jimmy asked.

Jeff continued. "He said some man was after him. But, he wouldn't tell us why."

With that Freddy started whimpering.

Uncle Jimmy crouched down and put his hands on Freddy's shoulders.

"It's OK, Freddy. I'm here and I won't let anyone hurt you. Now what happened?"

Freddy whimpered a little, then gathered his courage and began.

"This man came up to me. He was real friendly and wanted to know where I was goin' and how did I like school and stuff."

"OK. Then what happened? Why are you crying?" Uncle Jimmy was patient and kind, but he was confused by Freddy's response. Then he glanced at us, and a curious look came over him.

"Do you want to talk in the front room?"

Freddy, without looking at us, nodded his head. Uncle Jimmy straightened up. He was quite tall, over six feet. He put his hand on Freddy's shoulders.

"Come on in the front room. I was just finishing some drawings. We can talk in there. You boys get some milk. Your mom has a cake in there Jeffrey, cut a piece for you fellas."

This was probably the first and only time we were not interested in one of Aunt Monie's cakes. She was by far the best cook in the family and made the best cakes and pies in the world. But, for some reason, maybe concern or fear, we just weren't interested in cake. We watched Uncle Jimmy and Freddy walk down the hallway toward the front room. Because the sun was streaming through the front window, all we could see were their silhouettes as the tall man reached down and placed his hand on the little boy's shoulder to comfort him.

We sat huddled together on the couch, quiet, nervous, glancing at one another, then focusing quickly back to the front room. All we could see from our vantage point was the sun streaming through the open window. Everything was still. There was no movement except for the curtains that billowed from of a slight breeze.

The silence was broken by the crash of a table being overturned in the front room and the stomping of Uncle Jimmy's feet as he thundered out of the front room and down the hall.

He was cursing under his breadth.

"You boys stay here!" He pointed to the couch. "Stay right there and don't move!"

In my entire life I had never seen a truly angry man. I'd seen my dad and my Uncle Herman upset before, but this was different. Uncle Jimmy was furious. He was almost crying, he was so angry. He went into the front closet and grabbed a baseball bat, then ran past us and flew out of the back door. We heard it slam shut behind him. While all this as happening, the five of us sat on the dining room couch. We sat closely, right next to one another, our mouths open, our heads pivoting as we watched Uncle Jimmy run out of the apartment. After he left, Freddy walked into the dining room. His eyes were red as he wiped his face with the sleeve of his shirt.

We instantly jumped up from the couch and huddled around him.

"You OK?" "What did you tell him?" "Dag. I've never seen my dad like that before."

None of our questions were answered. I don't think any of us expected it after we had looked at Freddy, his eyes red and frightened.

"Your dad told me to stay with you fellas."

"Sure, OK. You want some cake?" Billy tried to comfort him.

"No, uh-uhhh." He spoke in a whisper.

We could hear Uncle Jimmy as he ran down the back steps.

"Hey, you home, Mr. Cage? Hey, hey. Yea, come on….I'll tell you.."

His words were muffled, as he continued explaining to Mr. Cage what had happened in the neighborhood. We could hear more screen doors slam shut and other steps pounding down the back steps. We ran to the back porch and watched as Uncle Jimmy and a couple of men ran into the alley. I felt scared, yet safe. My brothers, my cousins, and my friend Freddy stood together shoulder to shoulder watching as the men in our building went out to find whatever had threatened us.

They found him.

At dinner that evening we sat quietly. Mom and Dad glanced at each other. The food on the table, which normally disappeared very quickly, sat barely touched. Steam rose from the mashed potatoes; the pork chops rested on the serving plate in the middle of the table. Dad reached for the mashed potatoes.

Mom started, "Carol, boys, something happened today that we need to talk about."

Dad looked at us.

"There was a man in the neighborhood who tried to abduct, uhh, I mean, uhhmm, kidnap one of Artie's friends. We don't know what he was going to do but we're certain he was going to hurt him. Fortunately, you boys were thinking and got home with your cousins. Thank God your Uncle Jimmy was home."

Mom picked it up from there.

"Yes, we do thank God that no one was hurt. And we are really happy and proud that all of you got together to help your friend. I spoke with his mother and father and they told me to tell you and your cousins how happy and proud of all of you they are. You should also know that your Uncle Jimmy, Mr. Cage, and Mrs. Lee found the man."

Carol asked, "How did they find him? Was he the right person?"

"Yes, Carol, it was the right man. From what we understand, Mrs. Lee called around the neighborhood, and one of her friends had seen a strange-looking fellow she had never seen before. He fit the description that Freddy gave Uncle Jimmy."

As she explained all of this to us, a curious little smile forced its way through the seriousness of the moment and onto her lips.

"We also heard Mrs. Lee caught him. Evidently, they had spotted the idiot and started running after him. Mrs. Lee, still in her house shoes, outran all the men and caught up with him. She was able to knock him down. Then she whacked him upside the head with her trusty old broom…Darn it, that old woman sure can run!"

She shook her head, the smile still on her lips. Dad agreed.

"She surely can. Hey, Artie, hand me some of those mashed potatoes. I hope you folks aren't hungry, because for some reason, I am famished. I could eat everything on this table."

"Yea, me, too." "Me, too." "Me three." My brothers and I quickly grabbed for the food.

Pete then said, "Hey Carol, congratulations on making the cheerleading squad. I saw Sharon this afternoon and she told me about it. That's real cool."

That's when we noticed Carol's demeanor; she sat in her chair quietly. She didn't move. She was staring down at her empty plate, her hands folded in her lap. She was eerily quiet and still, except for her lips. She was fiercely biting them, she was angry.

"I hope they beat him….I hope they beat the…." She was going to say something else but her quivering lips cut off any other words.

Dad stopped eating and watched her, then he reached out and gently put his hand on hers.

"I know, honey… I think….. I believe he got the message. That… that. .animal will never come around here again."

Something cruel and mean and horrible had reached out and gotten very close to us. Fortunately, this time it had been dealt with and was now gone. For the moment our family and the neighborhood were safe from harm. We could all sleep well, without any fear of the night.

Chapter seven

The End of the Beginning

Winter arrived early in 1954, pushing past fall like a schoolyard bully, as the warm Indian summer gave way to a blast of unwelcome frigid air. A premature snow fell just before Halloween, snatching the last few leaves from the trees. Scattered up and down the street, piles of raked leaves were lined up, capped with several inches of snow, making the whole block look as though some benevolent giant had baked dozens of apple pies and topped them with whipped cream.

When we walked to school the Friday before Halloween, which was on Sunday, all any of us could talk about was what we were going to wear on Halloween, plus how much candy we were going to get from people. We also evaluated each neighbor on the kind and amount of candy each person gave.

"Yea, you can forget Mrs. Harris 'cause all they give are stupid apples and they are all brown and mushy." I remembered that from last year.

"Yea, the Melnicks gave some kinda popcorn balls last year. Yechhh!! I hate those things." Marty knew what he didn't like.

"I'm going to be a pirate," Billy suddenly proclaimed with a grin on his face. That, Jeffrey quickly and completely squelched.

"Billy, I told you I'm gonna be a pirate. You can be a bum. Heck, you're one already with those flap-flap shoes you got on." Jeffrey started grinning.

Flap-flap shoes were what often happened when the sole separated from the bottom of the front of our shoes but was still connected to the middle of the shoe. The sound that resulted when you walked with them was a flap-flap, flap-flap. Billy and Marty had this happen to them often, because most of their shoes were hand-me-downs from their older brothers. They were generally very, very worn when they finally got to them.

If our parents had enough money, they would have them re-soled, but until then, the only option we had was to tape them up or make due. Billy was going to have to make due for a while longer.

"No, I ain't no bum. I'm telling Mom. She said I was going to be the pirate this year. She told me you're too old to go trick or treatin' anyway."

"Yea, well, I'm not too old to get free candy, so you can just shut up about it." Jeffrey retorted.

"Pete, you going trick or treating, too, aren't you?" Jeff was looking for support.

"No, and neither are you." We all looked at Pete curiously.

"What do you mean? What are you talking about? I am too goin' trick or treatin.'"

"No, you're not. My dad said that all the grown ups decided that Mrs. Lee isn't going to get any peeing visitors this Halloween. They all had some kind of meeting and decided that we are going to have to help her from now on. They decided all this because she helped catch that creepy man that bothered Freddy Moore."

What was the most amazing thing to us was that the adults in our neighborhood had a meeting and we didn't know anything about it. We could live with preventing anyone from peeing on Mrs. Lee's front porch, but what was really difficult to accept was that the adults had gotten together and made a decision about us and we didn't know anything about it. That was truly frightening.

"Darn, nobody told me about that." Jeffrey was clearly dejected, when suddenly a light went on.

"Hey, Billy, you know I was just kidding about you being a pirate. Heck, I'll even help you with your costume."

Saturday morning Marty and I were up early, and Billy had already come upstairs to our apartment. We were excited about Halloween, and even though it came on a Sunday that year, we still started bragging about our costumes. The most important thing was to argue with each other about whose costume was going to be the best. I decided to be a clown again, even though I had been one before. Everyone made their own costumes, which kind of limited us to being a clown, a bum, a pirate, or a monster. Therefore, we had to be really creative so our costumes would be different. I tried to think of things that no one else had ever done or thought of before. I had picked out one of my dad's old ties and pants. I was going to put some of Mom's lipstick on my eyebrows and make one great big giant red one. I had already hollowed out a big dill pickle to make a big fake nose. I put a couple holes near the thick part of it, and tied a string around it so that it would fit snuggly on my face. It was about three inches long. I had thought of it myself and was quite proud of my invention. I had also decided on the clown's name, "Sir Pickle from Pluto." So, I pranced around our apartment proclaiming, "All the people on Earth are to be my subjects, for I am Sir Pickle-nose from Pluto!!"

Marty and Billy were rolling on the floor, cracking up.

Unfortunately, Pete walked into the dining room where we were and started laughing, too. Usually he was on the milk route with our father but had stayed home with a fake stomach ache. He had been listening and had heard what I had dubbed myself but had also made up an alternative name for me.

"Sir Knucklehead from Neptune. It is he, I do declare," he announced.

I ignored him, pretending I didn't care. I continued to prance around the room, but Marty and Billy were laughing even harder at Pete's new name for me. I stopped my solo parade, a bit dejected and said, "You're just mad cause you have to be on Pee Patrol tonight. You're just mad cause I get to go trick or treating and you can't."

I must have hit a nerve, because Pete paused a moment then looked at me and smiled. "Yea, you're right," he owned. "I guess I am. Hey, Art, that nose is pretty cool. Did you think of that by your-self?"

"Yep, I sure did. I needed a bigger nose and I couldn't figure any-thing out. I tried a toilet paper roll, but you could see my nose in the end of it. Then I just thought of a pickle."

"Yea, well you did a good job. That's really funny looking. Hey, let me try it on."

Pete validated my idea, and because he was the one I looked up to the most, his opinion was very important.

"Hey, Pete, me and Marty and Billy will give you some of our candy. Won't we, fellas?"

Billy and Marty had been quietly listening to Pete and me, but when I volunteered some of their candy, the silence ended.

"Uh-uhhh. No, we ain't." Billy quickly blurted.

"Me neither. I'm keepin' all my candy," Marty agreed.

Then with a mischievous smile, Marty added, "I'll give you some of my candy if you smell my stinky feet."

"I'll smell your stinky feet when you take them out of your mouth." Pete's attempt at a response was terrible. It was what we called "lame." And Marty, knowing he had the upper hand, didn't let up.

"Yep, and after you smell my stinky feet, you can make some toe-jam soup for dinner."

Marty was grinning from ear to ear, while Billy and I fell against one another cracking up. Even Pete started laughing at Marty's teas-ing.

When Halloween eve came, we were ready, all dressed up and out the door early. Marty, Billy, and I started trick or treating at the building on the corner of our block and decided to go down our street into each apartment building and down the other side of the street into each building. We figured we would get to at least 100 residences before we finished. Our moms had given us shopping bags for our candy, so we could collect a great supply of candy.

After a few hours of intense trick or treating, the three of us were excited with the amount of candy we had collected. We had a wonderful night with so many children, who were all out laughing and enjoying the fun. The streets were filled with every kind of creature and goblin, bums, clowns and princesses. Most were creatively designed, but because it was a cold fall evening, many costumes were hidden by overcoats.

We had just finished trick or treating in our building when we spotted Pete, Jeffrey, and Mickey sitting on the steps in front of Mrs. Lee's house. They were drinking something warm in cups that they cradled in their hands. You could see the steam rising up to their mouths as they took generous gulps of the warm liquid. They were standing guard against any wayward peeing.

"Hi, Mick. Hi, Jeff. Hi, Pete." Billy greeted them. "Whatcha drinking?"

Mickey was the first to speak. "It's hot cocoa. Mrs. Lee gave it to us. She said it was too cold to stand out here without something to warm your innards."

"She did, really? Wow, I wonder what's the matter with her?" Billy spoke for all of us.

"I don't think anything's wrong with her. She just came out and gave it to us." Jeff added.

"Have you stopped anyone from doing it on her porch yet?" Marty asked.

"Nah. Every kid that's been by so far knows what happened when she went upside that man's head last week, so nobody wants to mess with her anymore." Pete said matter-of-factly.

Jeffrey nodded his head in agreement. "Look what else she gave us."

Next to him was a huge paper bag. He put down his cup of cocoa, picked up the bag, and tilted it so we could see inside.

At first we were unable to see because it had gotten dark, but when we got closer and looked inside the bag, what we saw astounded us. Piled inside were dozens of candy bars and packs of gum, the best kind of stuff ever. There were Milky Ways, Musketeers, Junior Mints, Bazooka bubble gum, and Wrigley's chewing gum. We stood absolutely amazed.

"She didn't say anything except, 'Here. You are good boys,' then she closed the door and went inside."

"Wow! Can we trick or treat her?" Billy was impressed, but he understood the mission.

"Yea, go ahead" Mickey said.

We rang her bell, and when she came out, she smiled at us, then gave us each several bars of candy, which was the prized trick or treat target.

"Here you go, boys. Hope you like these." It was the first time we could remember her saying anything to us that wasn't a scream or yell.

"Yes, Ma'am. Thank you, thank you very much," we chorused.

"Man, when she smiled, I didn't even know it was her. I didn't even know she had any teeth," Marty laughed.

We vowed at that moment to be nice to her for the rest of our lives. As we finished trick or treating that cold evening, I walked home with my brother and cousin and a shopping bag full of candy. I knew that this Halloween was one of the best ever.

It was picture day at school that Monday after Halloween. That morning, Mom made us dress up in a shirt and tie for the photograph. We all put up a mild protest, but we really didn't mind. Most of the kids would be dressed up that day anyway. Every class would march down to the assembly hall and have their class pictures taken.

"I hope they don't make me sit on the floor as usual." Pete's concerns were shared by Marty and me as well. Because we were short, each of us had to sit on the floor, and usually in front of the girls for our class picture. Boys and girls were generally separated, not only by the entrances into the school building, but also in our school pictures.

Pete then told me something that was unbelievable.

"I asked Dad if he would let me wear his ring for the picture and he said yes. I think it's going to look real good, so I'm going to hold my hand out so people can see it."

"Really? You're going to do that? Wow, and Dad let you wear that ring?" I was amazed. Dad didn't usually let us use any of his things, like his socks or pencils that he had for work.

"Yep, he sure did."

We were at school for 15 minutes before Mrs. Seahigh escorted us down to the assembly hall. There were two classes already there.

I saw Marty's class as they left the cavernous room. I couldn't get his attention because he was talking to one of his friends, and the assembly hall was noisy with the chatter of so many children.

After we filed into the hall, we sat behind the other classes that had gotten there before us. A group of students was moving onto the stage, and a few had already stepped onto a riser placed right in front of a huge camera. It sat atop a wooden tripod. The photographer stood next to it while he ushered wondering children to their proper places, trying to get them to move more quickly than they were.

"C'mon, children, please move faster. I have to take a lot of pictures today. Now, you shorter boys wait for the taller kids to step up on the riser. That's right. No, you boys wait a minute. There you go. Yep, no. Yes that's right. Stop. Wait, young man. Wait, don't go up there. You're going to sit on the floor. You're not tall enough…."

I didn't hear the rest of what he said because the boy he was talking to was Pete. I watched as Pete stepped back and let the taller kids go to the top of the riser. He stood to the side, trying to become invisible. Jeffrey and Bo walked over to talk to him. Pete looked embarrassed. Then, the photographer continued.

"Excuse me, young man. You can go up to the next row." He was talking to Bo. "Now you and you. OK. Yes. You next." He was pointing to Jeffrey.

"All right, now, girls, you go sit in the chairs. OK. Yep, that's right. Just file in. OK. Good job. OK. Now you shorter boys sit on the floor right in front of the girls. OK, good. Keep moving. All right. Yep, you, yea, sit right there on the end. Good. Now hold still everyone. Hold still…look this way. Hold still… Now smile, smile big."

Click. The big camera's shutter signaled the end of the session. The kids reacted immediately and scrambled quickly to their feet. Pete, however, got up very, very slowly. I watched as Jeffrey and Bo swiftly moved to get in line next to him. I noticed that Bo said something to him and Pete reacted by holding out his hand. Bo and Jeffrey looked at Pete's ring and nodded their heads smiling. I couldn't really see him, because his head was turned away from me, but I believe that Pete smiled, too. He left with his class, and he didn't notice me, because I didn't wave at him. I never told him I had seen what happened on that picture day.

When my class was finally called up, I was seated on the floor in front of the girls, too. I accepted my plight and smiled when the click came that signaled my release. I hustled to my feet, trying to mix in with the taller boys, brushing off my pants so that no one could see the tale-tale smudges I got from the dusty floor. I was surprised that no one talked about where they had to stand, or sit, while their picture was taken. I was glad, though.

That evening, the talk at the dinner table was normal. Another picture day was over, and we had made it through another humiliating ordeal. I never mentioned to Pete that I saw him. I don't know why not, then again, maybe I do. Well, it was over now and I thought to myself, "Thank God."

My family's routine of school, play, and work whittled away the days. And before most adults were ready, Christmas was upon us.

December was only a week away when Marty, Pete, and I began working feverishly on our Christmas lists.

"I'm gonna get a Schwin bicycle and an Erector set. That's what I want the most." Pete was excited.

"I want a Bozo the Clown punching bag." Marty had seen one in a catalog.

"I'm gettin' some Lincoln logs and a Mr. Potato head." I had wanted these toys for a long time.

"I can hear you boys in there. Do you think you deserve such wonderful gifts from Santa Claus?"

Pete and I looked awkwardly at one another, knowing that Marty, who would be turning seven just before Christmas, still believed in Santa Claus. So we sat unsure of how to respond. After an uneasy moment, Marty baled us out with a great answer.

"Heck yea, Mom, as long as you think so!"

Mom, who was in the kitchen making breakfast, peered in at us with a curious look on her face. We just smiled at her, and then turned our attention back to what was really important, our Christmas lists.

"One of you boys go wake up your sister for breakfast." Mom asked from the kitchen. We didn't move, looking at one another, waiting.

"You go, Marty." "Yea, you go, Marty," Pete and I ganged up on our younger brother.

"Uh-uhhh. I'm not going. You two get her." Marty was standing up for himself.

"Stop it! Artie, you go wake her up." Mom's voice overpowered the sound of her cooking.

"Me? Why me?" I got up off the floor where we had been writing our lists.

"Because I said so," Mom answered in the way I hated the most. She didn't usually answer that way; only Dad did, so we knew Mom was irritated.

But before I could take a step, Carol walked in from the living room where she slept.

"That's OK, Mom. I'm up. And a happy good morning to you, my knuckleheaded brothers."

Carol sauntered into the dining room and stretched leisurely.

"The life of a cheerleader is certainly difficult." With exaggeration she stepped past us and into the kitchen to help Mom with breakfast. She had been quite the princess the last month or so. She had gradually let go the anger at the man who had scared Freddy Moore a couple months previous. For whatever reason, it was very difficult for her to accept that people like that were walking around our neighborhood or any neighborhood, for that matter.

"Well, Miss High and Mighty, would your graciousness please take the garbage out?" Mom's request to Carol came with a deep bow as she pointed to the bags of garbage that Pete and I had not taken out yet.

"Maaaaaaaaaaaaaa!" Carol's wale of discuss lasted at least 30 seconds. "That's the boys' job!!" she pleaded.

"Carol, do as I say," Mom was unrelenting. We were cracking up. Deep tear-bringing laughs. Unfortunately, Mom heard us and decided on a special task for us.

"Boys, and I mean all three of you, go make up Carol's bed and put it in the closet. Your Uncle Herman and Aunt Chris are coming over this evening and we need to clean up."

"Maaaaaaaaaaaaaaa! That's Carol's job." Our laughs were quickly smothered by angst. The resonance of our disgust sounded like a choral arrangement by the Vienna Boys Choir.

Carol slept on a roll-away bed in the living room. Putting it away required that we fold the sheets and blankets neatly, lift the ends of the bed up, then latch it at the top with the metal hook-and-eye. The bed was on wheels so it could be pushed into the front closet for storage during the day.

"Boys, do as I say." As Mom responded, like we knew she would, we spotted Carol behind her. She was smiling at us with her eyes crossed. She was really enjoying this. We grumbled among ourselves as we trudged into the living room.

"I wish all those boys who think she's so cute could see her in the morning." Pete sneered "Yea, me, too." "Me three." Marty and I agreed.

Truth was, we adored our older sister, and for good reason. She was a fountain of information who knew all the cool songs and dances, not that we would ever want to dance, or even touch a girl. We were really intrigued by Carol. We often sat in the living room and watched as she twirled around, practicing dance steps with imaginary boys, her "Prince Charming," as she called them.

Carol was also very quick to defend us. She was nearly six feet tall when she was only 13 and was quite a tomboy before she turned into a cheerleader. But, we were still not afraid to call on her if we got in trouble or were picked on by some neighborhood bully. One time in particular was quite funny.

Earlier in the year, right before the broken window incident at Mr. Malarcher's garage, Marty, Billy, and I were playing in the back when one of our friends came into the yard and wanted to play with us. He was with a really big boy whom we didn't know; who he said was his older cousin from East St. Louis, a town a few hundred miles south of Chicago. We were just playing catch at the time, so we gladly included them. The rubber ball we used bounced well, and we liked catching ground balls. We threw the ball on the ground so we could scoop it up with our bare hands and then quickly toss it to someone else. Usually we included the required play-by-play, at which Billy was quite adept.

Billy threw a grounder to me.

"Ground ball to Artie. Picks it up. Over to Marty. The runner's outtttttt!"

Marty then threw it to Frankie, our friend, who knew our routine. He deftly scooped the ball up and threw it to his cousin, who was rather clumsy. He missed it, then dropped it, then kicked it, then dropped it again. Billy continued with his play-by-play.

"Ground ball to Frankie. Picks it up. Over to.... Drops the ball! Drops it again! Now kicks it. Drops it again. Falls on it. Rolls over it. Puts it in his pocket and poops on it!!"

Marty and I were dying, we were figuratively dying. I couldn't see, I was cracking up so much. Marty was rolling around on the ground, his face distorted in laughter, his mouth wide open. He was laughing so hard no sound was coming out. It was truly hilarious. Hilarious until we looked at Frankie's cousin, who was embarrassed. His eyes were tearing up. I don't know if he was crying from anger or embarrassment, but one thing was clear—he was getting mad.

"You better shut up, man. Ain't nothin' funny!!" His teeth were clenched, as were his fists.

"That's cause you can't see you." Billy's quick wit did not make the big boy very happy.

"Oh, yea? I bet I can make you eat this ball with my fist!" This was said with his fist balled up and held menacingly in Billy's direction. Then he began slowly closing in on a startled Billy.

"Hey, man, I'm just kiddin'," Billy said, backing up. He realized too late that he had irritated the much larger boy. "Frankie, tell him I was jut kiddin'."

"Tommy, Billy is just teasin'. Don't bother him," Frankie said.

"Yea, well, he was laughin' before, but he ain't laughin' now, and when I'm done beatin' him up, he won't be laughin' later."

Marty and I tried to stop him. "You better not bother him. He's our cousin." We said it as menacingly as we possibly could. Other than fighting with one another, none of us had ever been in a real fight.

"Oh, don't you two worry. I saw you laughin'. When I'm done with him, I'm getting you, too."

Things got serious very quickly. This boy was older than we and was six inches taller.

At that precise moment, everything stopped. Even the boy who was menacing us stopped dead in his tracks. A sound literally slammed through the neighborhood. It was so piercing, it could have broken glass. We stood there transfixed by the cold-blooded yet strangely human sound. Then, slowly, like the echo of a close friend's footsteps, I realized that this inhuman screech had a strange familiarity. IT WAS CAROL. She was flying down the back steps. And she was screaming. No, she wasn't screaming. That's not it. She was bellowing. Bellowing like a million screech owls whose chicks have been threatened. It was the most remarkable sound I had ever heard a human being emit.

"Dooon't you tooouuuchhhh themmmm! I will gettttttt yoo-ouuuu! I'mmm commmmmminnnggg!"

I had never seen anyone change right before my eyes until that day. This huge kid who was about to trounce us turned into a frightened little bird. He saw her coming, and the way she looked was as frightening as the sounds she was making. He turned around and took off, running as fast as character in a Bugs Bunny cartoon. The three of us had gone from being completely frightened that we were about to get whupped to being amused and relieved that our tormentor had turned into a scared little boy.

We were so relieved, our knees were shaking and we had to sit on the ground.

When Carol reached the bottom of the steps and sprinted into the yard, it was empty except for us. She finally stopped and after a moment of catching her breath, she calmed down.

"I was standing on the back porch watching when I saw that kid bothering you boys. Sorry I had to scream like that." She looked at us with her crooked smile. "Frankie, is that a friend of yours?"

Frankie was standing there, his mouth open. After a moment he shook his head and muttered, almost inaudibly, "He used to be my cousin."

Carol's legend took on a whole new meaning after that day, and it grew and grew.

So moving her bed from the living room into the closet was not as distasteful as we pretended.

That evening and several evenings on, around, and during Christmas, our home was filled with relatives and friends. We celebrated the joy of Christmas and the love of family.

Usually during the season we would see all of our cousins—the Jacksons, the Plotts, the Smiths, all of them. It was always a happy and joyful season in the Miller household. Santa usually brought us most of the toys we asked for, and this Christmas was no different.

After Christmas the rest of winter was a blur. The New Year came quickly and passed quickly. Before long, spring arrived and with it came a week's vacation from school. But, it was not really a vacation. During the 1950s each student throughout the city was expected to get involved in a neighborhood cleanup project. In the spring of 1955, Mrs. Seahigh's class was assigned a vacant lot on Eberhardt Ave., the street where Mr. Hamilton's store was located.

We were expected to be at the cleanup site at 8:00 that Monday morning. Nearly every student was there on time, and so was Mrs. Seahigh. She had on a huge pair of grey men's overalls. It was the most incredible thing any of us had ever seen. There she was, in men's overalls! It was amazing, a teacher, especially Mrs. Seahigh in overalls. Most of us just stared at her in disbelief. She looked like an old farmer or something. We all just cracked up, the boys especially.

After an inordinate amount of time and the appropriate amount of laughing and pointing, we bent to the task of cleaning up the vacant lot.

It was not as repulsive as I first thought. It actually became a lot of fun. Much of the fun we had may have been because of the daily appearance of Mrs. Seahigh in one strange getup after another. None of her elaborate wear gave any hint of her profession as a teacher.

We all found her to be rather human, a fact that we would have never been convinced of earlier in the semester. Seeing her in a different setting allowed us to see her differently. That, and Mr. Malarcher showed up to help us. He would never allow any of the children to giggle at Mrs. Seahigh's appearance. I'm not sure what it was about him, but without speaking, he demanded and received deep respect from everyone around him.

At the end of that spring cleanup week, we had picked up a pile of discarded bottles, cans, and paper that people had carelessly discarded. Several other adults in the neighborhood besides Mr. Malarcher also volunteered in cleaning up the alleys and empty lots. The whole area looked sparkling clean; it looked nice. I loved the neighborhood.

The last days of school before summer vacation were the best part of going to school. The anticipation of a long, warm, happy summer was often more fulfilling than the reality of it.

"We're going to Three Rivers, Michigan, for the summer." Pete was as excited as Marty and I as he shared our family's plans as we and our friends walked home on the last day of school.

"I'm finally getting a chance to go and visit my Grandpa in Mississippi." Emmett was ecstatic. He had tried to convince his mom that he would be fine if she let him go to Mississippi by himself.

"You fellas wou..wouldn't believe how country some of my cousins are. Most of the time they don't even wear shoes—just go around bare foot."

"Mississippi. My mom says that things are different down there." Jeffrey was shaking his head. Looking down at his shoes, he kicked at something no one else could see.

"Man, what do they do in the winter time?" Jeff was honestly curious.

"Jeez ,Jeffrey, they don't have cold winters in Mississippi. It's always hot."

"Oh. Then don't their feet get hot on the sidewalks?" Jeff's logic was understandable.

"No, everything is dirt. There ain't no sidewalks. Mississippi is the country, the real country. I'm not going until August anyway. I'll probably see you around before I go. Hey, you fellas have a good summer. Re..re..remember, next year is our last year in grammar school. See ya, Artie. Watch out for broken windows." Bo liked kidding me about our experience at Mr. Malarcher's garage.

"Yea. Have a good summer, Bo. See ya. Bye. Bye." We all waved as he headed for his apartment on St. Lawrence. We turned for home, not knowing that this would be the last time we would ever see him alive. It then started raining, so we ran home as fast as we could.

Pete Miller first boy seated left 1st row

Jeffrey Green second boy from left 3rd row

Emmett Till sixth boy from left 3rd row

Chapter eight

Comes the Rain

We were leaving for Michigan in August, which was a little later than we usually went, but my parents couldn't get their vacations until later that summer. My brothers and I became excited when the time to leave for the farm got close. We eagerly anticipated the joy of being in the "country."

"I'm goin' to go fishin' everyday." Marty's favorite thing to do was fish. He wasn't very successful, but he truly loved it. Billy and I watched as Marty mimicked his fishing technique on the back porch one evening before we left.

"I sure wish I was goin' too, but Mom said I had to stay home." Billy was really dejected. He and his brothers came with us often. But this summer Aunt Monie had made other plans. My brothers and I were also a bit dejected. The fact that our cousins weren't going to join us muffled our excitement. When the six of us were on the farm, it was exhilarating. We had acres upon acres of open countryside to play in, streams to splash in, and trees to climb. We embraced the joy and freedom of melding with the openness and purity of nature. Unfortunately, they weren't going to join us that summer.

My brothers and I were up early the morning we left for Michigan, and we didn't sleep well the night before. As was usual, everything was chaotic. Pete, Marty, and I were getting in each other's way, laughing and tripping each other. We packed all of our clothes in pillowcases; wrinkles, we figured, were a fashion statement. Mom didn't care as long as we were clean. Eventually we made it down to the car, following appropriate goodbyes to our sister, who couldn't go with us because of a summer class she was taking, we began our trip to Michigan. As we left home, our laughter slowly subsided. The ride to our get-away took three hours, it always seemed longer.

The first thing I always noticed when we drove onto the driveway was the sound. I loved the noise the tires made as they rolled over the gravel driveway. My Uncle Herman had spread the gravel onto the dirt driveway beside the old farmhouse a few years earlier. Before the gravel had been laid, the car would sink hopelessly into thick mud whenever it rained. The sound made as the tires rode over the stones was familiar and comforting. It has always reminded me of joyous, warm summer days spent in Michigan.

As we escaped from the cramped car, we rushed to the house. We loved the old clapboard building. It had been built in the 1920s, just before the Great Depression. It was painted a stark white that was faded by time. The house been built to withstand the cold Michigan winters. It was what my mom called "sturdy." The musty smell that flooded our senses reminded me of my grandmother's closet. But that smell quickly faded when we got there. We brought the smell of young life.

The farmhouse normally stayed vacant—vacant until we arrived. Our neighbors who lived a mile down the road would look in on the house from time to time to make certain nothing was amiss. In return they were given the freedom to plant their crops on 40 of the 80 acres my parents and uncle owned. Even though the neighboring farmer felt he should share the profit from the crops he planted on our land, my family did not require such payment. We felt our neighbors watching out for our property was payment enough

The first morning after we had gotten to the farm, my brothers and I woke up early, before Mom and Dad had stirred. The house was still, and quiet, as we slipped out of our beds and dressed quickly. Our plan was to walk down the road to the small stream that ran near the house and go fishing. The night before, we had laid out the three fishing poles that were stored at the house. We had also gone out when it was dark and captured huge night-crawler worms for bait. We hoped they would be very tempting for a lot of hungry fish. We quickly ate some cereal for breakfast before Mom and Dad woke up and were out the screened back door in a flash. We went down the driveway and down the dirt road toward the nearby stream, dragging our fishing equipment behind us as we made our way to the bridge that straddled the little river. This was the spot we fished from every summer. Our vacation had officially begun when three red bobbers floated to the surface of that little creek.

The days drifted together. We played in the woods and we hunted and fished. We loved to visit an old country store down route 60 near our house. The people who owned it, Mr. and Mrs. Brown, weren't very receptive to our visits, but we usually ignored their rudeness and bought the candy and popsicles we liked so much. At night we roasted marshmallows on huge bonfires in a pit my father dug behind the house. It was an extraordinary escape from the crowded city where our neighbors lived within inches of us and where everything was concrete. At the farm, the green was almost blinding, the silence nearly deafening. The stars in the night sky were beyond description. My mother explained it perfectly. "Only God can create such beauty."

The first time I remember hearing her say this was one night as we sat around a bonfire roasting hotdogs and marshmallows. We stuck them on long sticks that were pulled from the walnut tree that grew near the house. I believe my mother was speaking of the beautiful black night, but then, maybe not.

We lived well and laughed often nearly everyday of that vacation.

August 31, 1955, was another typically beautiful late summer morning near the end of our vacation. I was awakened by the crowing of a far-off rooster. His enthusiastic call pierced my dreams as I quietly came out of my sleep. I sat up and saw that Marty was quietly snoring next to me. Pete wasn't there. He evidently had gotten up very early. I was excited because we had planned to hike into the woods behind the house to search for snakes. I stretched and yawned. I could see through the window in our bedroom that the day seemed nice. There were a few clouds, and I hoped for a warm and sunny day.

Then a scream came from the kitchen. It was deep and long and guttural. It sounded like a small animal that had been caught in a relentless steel trap. I scrambled out of the bed to find out what was happening. Marty sat up, jarred awake.

"Artie, what was that?"

"I don't know. I think it was Pete. C'mon."

We ran to the kitchen, but our parents had gotten there before us. Mom was hovering over Pete, who had his head buried in his arms on the kitchen table. Dad was leaning over him, next to Mom, trying to figure out what was wrong.

"Pete, what's wrong? What's wrong?" I yelled as I ran into the kitchen.

He slowly lifted his head, turned, and looked at me. His eyes were red, his mouth bent in a grotesque grimace. Hesitatingly, he spoke, not much louder than a whisper.

"Th-th- the paper, said... that Bobo got killed."

Artie and Marty Miller on the Michigan farm, late August, 1955

Chapter nine

Suffering Without Hope

As my dad slowly drove down the street to our home the day after we read about Emmett being killed, I looked at the place I knew so well. Even the buildings seemed as if they had been crying. A slight rain had fallen, and the streets gave off vapors that made everything seem heavy. The stately elm trees that lined the streets were bent over, saddened by the all the ugliness that had been unearthed and freed to contaminate the world.

None of our friends were outside; the streets seemed lonely. In our neighborhood, even when it was raining, someone would usually be outside, either playing or sitting on their front porch. Strangely, the street was vacant. No one was out, not even Mr. Malarcher, who was always in his yard. After the car was parked, and we got out there was an eerie quiet. It was like a movie where everyone had disappeared except for an unsuspecting family. It was odd.

Dad sighed. "Well, boys, I'll open the trunk. Let's see how much we can get upstairs in one trip."

His forced smile didn't ring true. The sadness in the air hungrily consumed any happiness or joy that surfaced.

Mom, who had been very quiet on the three-hour drive home, broke her silence.

"I'm going to run upstairs and find Carol." She said this over her shoulder without waiting for a response. She hurried down the sidewalk to the apartment building and rushed in to embrace her only daughter.

After finally removing everything from the trunk, we began carrying it up to our apartment. On our way up Aunt Monie opened her apartment door. She had changed in the three weeks we had been gone. She had gotten visibly older. Her once-round cheeks had fallen and her eyes had lost their sparkle. She looked dreadful.

Pete also noticed. Without thinking he said, "Aunt Monie? Aunt Monie, are you all right? Did something else happen?"

With words that carried ancient pain, she answered him. "No, Pete...not yet."

"We'll see you later." With that, Marty and Pete hurried upstairs. I was behind, Dad so I waited with him while he spoke to Aunt Monie.

"Hello, Ramona." Dad always called Aunt Monie Ramona. "How are you and the boys doing?"

"It's been difficult for everyone. They are really shaken, just like everyone else on the street. It's good to have you all back home. Have you seen Carol yet? I know she is upset. I thought I heard Helen. Did she go upstairs?" Aunt Monie asked everything in one breath.

"Yes, she just ran up, and no, I have not seen Carol yet. Did she stay with you last night?"

"No, I asked her if she wanted to, but she decided to stay upstairs. She did eat with us though. She was quiet….this whole thing has been so horrible," Aunt Monie said sadly.

"Have you heard anything about what happened yet?" Dad asked, putting down the boxes he was carrying.

"No, but we all know who it was…it had to be the Klan," she said, shaking her head. Just then Billy peeked from behind his mother's housedress. He was sucking his thumb, a habit he had broken a while back.

"Hi, Billy." My dad looked down at his nephew. "How ya doin'?" Dad was gentle.

"Ok," Billy answered behind his thumb. He smiled, his thumb still in his mouth. He waved at me with his other hand.

"Warren !?" Mom's call came from the floor above.

"I'm coming up, honey!" Dad answered.

"All right. Carol wants you!" Mom went back into our apartment.

"I'll see you later," Dad said to Aunt Monie as he picked up the boxes.

"OK. Tell Helen I'll be up when you all get settled. We need to talk." She pulled Billy in and quietly closed the door. I didn't go upstairs with my brothers because I wanted to tell my father something while we were alone. As we walked up the last flight of stairs, I took a chance.

"Dad?" I mumbled.

"Yea, Art."

"I'm sacred," I confessed.

"I know, son, but try to understand. We'll be OK. I know you and Carol and your brothers...your mom...and me, too—we're all frightened. All this stuff...it's hard to deal with. I mean, this is too close to home. But we, all of us, are going to somehow be OK."

Dad had stopped before we had gotten to the top of the stairs and was looking down at me.

"This isn't going to be easy. I can't even begin to know how Emmett's mom must be feeling. We...I can't believe that...we just got to ...do something."

For the first time in my 10 years, I felt I really needed to hug my father, but not for me—for him.

He looked out the hallway window and was quiet for a moment, then remembered he had a daughter he hadn't seen. He turned quickly and ran up the last few steps.

"Artie, make sure the windows in the car are rolled up. I think it's still raining." Dad had stopped as he entered the apartment, tried a little smile, then went quickly inside. I heard him calling for my sister.

I dropped the box of clothing and ran downstairs. As I hurried down to the car, I saw Frances. She was sitting on the steps right outside her apartment. She hadn't been there when we came in.

I noticed smudges on her cheeks. She had been crying.

"Hi, Artie. I was sitting at our front window when I saw you and your family drive up. I needed…" She hesitated, not knowing how to express her feelings.

I sat on the step next to her. I was not afraid to look at her as I sometimes was. She looked very small, smaller than I remembered.

"Hi." I whispered. We just sat there, not speaking, but receiving some kind of comfort without talking. It was at least five minutes before she spoke.

"Do you think we're gonna be all right?"

I didn't know what to say. I was scared of what was in the neighborhood. Fear was invading everything I cared about…fear was invading everything that protected me.

Not knowing what else to say, but realizing I had to be brave, I said, "Yes Frances, I think everything's gonna be OK."

She looked at me for a long time. I don't think she believed me. The slight sound of tumblers being released preceded the apartment door opening.

"Frances." It was her mother, Mrs. Cage. "Oh, hi, Artie. I see you and your family are home. I'm glad you're back. Tell your mom and dad that I'll be talking to them tonight about a meeting, a meeting about Mrs. Till, OK?"

"Yes, ma'am, I will."

"Frances, you come inside when you two are finished talking." She looked down at her daughter. There was a close bond between the two of them. I had noticed it before.

"Yes, Mama." Frances tried a weak smile. "I will."

Mrs. Cage closed the door, leaving us sitting alone in the hallway.

"She doesn't let me out of her sight anymore." Frances then exhaled a deep sigh.

We sat a little longer, not talking, just sitting together quietly. After a while, maybe five minutes, she got up to go into her apartment. I remained seated as she stood and gathered her skirt around her legs. She was standing motionless next to me when she slowly turned toward me, touched my shoulder, and then leaned over and kissed me on my cheek. The feeling of her lips touching me remained long after she quietly walked into her apartment.

I sat on the shadowed steps of our apartment building, stunned. I touched my cheek where she had kissed me. The tender gesture frightened me, and I didn't know why, but I realized one thing—I would never forget that moment.

"Artie. Artie!" It was Carol. She was leaning over the second-floor banister, looking down at me. "Hi. Are you OK? When you didn't come up, I got a little worried."

"Hi…. No…I'm OK."

"Artie, what's the matter?" She started down the stairs.

I'm unsure why it happened then, but the sheer tragedy of all that had taken place hit me. I flew up the remaining stairs that separated my sister and me and fell into her arms. I began to cry. I shed tears that came from the deepest part of my being. I cried fully as my sister held me. I cried for her. I cried for my cousins. I cried for my brothers. I cried for my parents. I cried because Frances kissed me. I cried for my neighborhood. I cried because I couldn't do anything else. I cried for Emmett. I cried because he was a little boy like me. I cried in my sister's arms because there was an ugliness in the world that I couldn't understand. I cried because Carol couldn't protect me. I could feel her arms around me, but I was still scared. She didn't say anything; she just clung to me, holding me as I trembled in her embrace. I realized then that she was crying, too.

My memory of the next few days is hazy, though I do remember that most everyone seemed out of sorts, as if in a fog. The adults in the community raised money to help bury Emmett. They had meetings about what could be done, about ways to voice our concerns and anger with Emmett's death to the government. Much was done to protest the brutality of his murder. For our parents, Emmett became a symbol of the persecution Negroes had to endure in the South as well as the North. His death made them realize that the tragedy that was happening in the South was also happening to black people in the North. It took the death of another innocent child for them to realize that they weren't as free as they thought they were.

The funeral for our friend was huge. I was unsure if some attended only because of the notoriety of his death. The Saturday the funeral began, I talked with Mom about it.

"Mom, I saw in the newspaper that Bo's funeral is today."

"Yes, it is. I spoke with Mrs. Lee, and she said they expect it to be several days."

"Are you and Dad going?" I asked.

"I am, but I don't think your father is going. Why, honey?" she asked.

"Well, Mom. I don't think Bo knew all these people. Why... How come they're going to his funeral?"

Mom and I were in the kitchen. She was washing dishes, and I was helping by drying them and putting them away. She stopped and wiped her hands on her apron, then exhaled a deep, long sigh.

"Artie, even though people didn't know him, they need to have a way to express their anger and concern about what happened to him. They also want to show their support for Emmett's mom. This is very hard for everyone around here. I know that this terrible thing is hard for Pete, and for you, because you knew him. Remember when we were at the farm? I tried to explain the way things are for Negroes, and that it might be too hard for you to understand."

She stopped a moment and put her hand on my shoulder. She sighed again, gathering her thoughts as she turned and hugged me. I could feel her heart beating against my face.

"I am old, sweetheart, and I don't understand how some people can hate so much, but it is clear that many do."

She looked down at me and smiled.

"Artie, I love you. Your dad and I will do anything to try and protect you...to protect all of you from ever being hurt. I promise you that."

I stood in my mother's embrace, listening to her heart and believing her.

We finished washing the dishes. I dried them and put them away without breaking anything.

When Mom decided that my brothers and I could not go to Bo's funeral, I was relieved. I was afraid to go, afraid of seeing him dead.

I learned later that almost every adult in the neighborhood attended, as did many of our friends.

My mother and sister went and were silent about what they had seen when they returned home. I only remember their eyes, which were red and swollen, and empty.

"Mom, Emmett's mother, did you hear what she said?" Carol's question fell from lips that trembled over a troubled thought.

Mom and Carol sat on the living room couch. Carol had her head on Mom's shoulder. It appeared as if they couldn't, or maybe wouldn't, separate themselves from one another. It was as if they drew strength and courage from their collective grief.

"Yes, Carol, I was close, so I heard her," she said "'The world needs to see what they did to my baby. They need to see what hate looks like.'"

Mom sighed with pain only a mother could know. She held my sister as she wept.

"That is the most courageous woman I have ever known."

That was the only conversation I heard from my mother regarding Bo's funeral. She, however, held his mother in high regard, mentioning her often when the subject of courage and conviction came up.

School started just about the same time funeral was ending. Several of my classmates who had attended the funeral talked about it.

"…It was really crowded, there were so many people there…." I heard Freddy Moore talking to some of the kids in our fifth-grade class.

"My mom and dad didn't let me go. They said it was too gruesome." Stephen Christmas, another classmate, seemed sorry that he wasn't allowed to attend Emmett's funeral.

"Bo lived two houses down from me." Stephen continued, then hesitated. He was going to say something else but chose not to. About five of us were standing around the room. We all were quiet. It seemed the whole world was quiet.

On the way to school that morning, I didn't hear the low hum of children's voices from a few blocks away as was normal. Instead, there was an eerie silence. It was the same silence that had lived on our street since Emmett's death.

As we stood around the classroom quietly waiting for new fifth-grade teacher, Mrs. Lindsey, she quietly entered the room. We must have startled her because her head was down when she walked in. I don't think she actually saw us, she seemed preoccupied. In one hand she had a rather large satchel and in the other, a handkerchief. She had just finished wiping her face when she realized her classroom was filled with thirty-odd students, some sitting, some standing, all looking to her for normalcy.

"Good morning, children." she offered.

Our obligatory "Good morning Mrs. Lindsey," lacked joy.

"Please find a seat on your own. Most of you have been together in class since kindergarten, so you should be able to seat yourselves alphabetically. I'll give you a few minutes to do that, while I get my desk in order. Thank you."

She then busied herself removing pencils, rulers, erasers, and other school material from a satchel she had carried in with her.

We stood silently for a split second, and then Stephen Christmas walked over to the first row to find his place. When he moved, we all began trying to find where our places were. I knew that my seat would be somewhere in the middle row. As I was moving toward the center of the classroom, I felt a tap on my shoulder. I turned around and looked into the soft eyes of my friend Freddy.

"I'm right behind you, Artie." He smiled. It was the first real smile I had seen for a long time. "School's started," he said.

And that was it. Mrs. Lindsey took attendance and told us what was expected of us as fifth graders. We had recess at 9:15, and then lunch at 12:00, and at 3:00 school was let out. Everything was supposed to go back to normal like nothing had happened, but something had.

Emmett's name was never mentioned at school by a teacher. Any comforting or counseling any child may have needed had to come from home. If it didn't happen there, it didn't happen at all.

The whole neighborhood followed the trial of the men who were accused of murdering Emmett. The trial was covered thoroughly in the *Chicago Defender* newspaper and on the radio. The adults all predicted that no Southern jury would ever convict white men of killing a young Negro boy. We, the young people, didn't believe that they could not. The adults were right and the young people were wrong.

On Friday, September 23, 1955, in Mississippi, J.W. Milam and Roy Bryant were acquitted of the murder of "Bo" Emmett Till, age 14, an eighth-grader at McCosh Elementary School.

Chapter ten

Suffering With Hope

"Mom, how could they do that?" Pete was trapped between the twin demons of anger and pain.

"It's not fair. It's just not fair!" His anguished wail fell into my mother's soul.

"No, baby, it's not fair. It's not fair at all." Mom lamented, unable to soothe her son's agony.

My brother's cry of pain and my mother's anguished response reflected the truth of America. The greatest country in the world tolerated the greatest injustices in the world.

The stage had finally been set. The unjust ruling had been given, and America had to face the truth because the world was watching. The United States could no longer close its eyes to its own peoples' plight.

The Negro community began to awaken and respond to the national disgrace of its own brutalization. Organizations like the NAACP and the Urban League grew dramatically in membership, and new organizations arose. They were created to fight the common enemy—that enemy was injustice and hatred. A collective resolve began to emerge; it was time to take a stand.

Little did the brutal men who stole a little boy from his grandfather's home recognize that their evil act, spurred the people they hated so much to become the greatest they had ever been. It obligated black people to stand up and fight for the rights they had long been denied.

Exactly 100 days after the death of Emmett, another woman who had the courage of Mrs. Till, took a extraordinary stand. Rosa Parks, after an exhausting day, refused to relinquish her seat to a white man. Her arrest in Montgomery, Alabama, spurred a protest against the racist policies that stained the United States of America. It has been said that Mrs. Parks remarked that her soul had been shaken by the murder of that little boy from Chicago, Emmett Till.

On the stormy evening of Sunday, December 4th, 1955, in Montgomery, Alabama, from the pulpits of their churches, the ministers who had met and organized declared "enough," and the boycott of the city buses began. It rained fully when the church bells rang and a people finally stood up.

A very young preacher came to the forefront of that courageous action—Dr. Martin Luther King, Jr. He was elected president of The Montgomery Improvement Association that sponsored the boycott.

From 1955 through the spring of 1957, we watched as black people began a dramatic transformation. My family—my mother in particular—made certain all of us realized what was happening to our people. A sense of my race and the implications of being a Negro filled me with pride. I was a part of a people that had endured, despite the tragic circumstances of its existence in America.

One Saturday afternoon in the summer of 1956, my mother and father were arguing over my mother's need to be involved in the burgeoning movement.

"Warren, I work also and contribute to this household, and I don't care that you think this is not going to help. As far as I'm concerned, I am writing this check to that church!"

My mother didn't stand up to my father very often, so it was amazing to hear how strongly she defended her position.

My father protested, "I think you are wasting our money and your time. Those white folk down there are never gonna let Negroes sit in the front row of those buses!"

"Well, that may be true. God knows how evil some of those people are, but I am going to do this. I'm going to do this for our children. I'm doing this for me. I'm doing this for Emmett's mama. And, Warren, I'm doing this for you, too." My mother tried a slight smile trying to get my dad to understand.

"Well, you may be doing that for a lot of reasons, but you're not doing it for me!"

With that said, Dad got up and walked out the door. Mom watched him leave and made no effort to go after him. Marty and I had been watching from the dining room, wondering what we could do. Meantime, Mom sat, shook her head slightly, then picked up her pen and continued writing in their checkbook.

Marty was the first to speak. "Mom, is Dad really mad at you?"

"Yes, honey, I guess he is." She was quiet a moment as she wrote the address on an envelope. When she had completed it, she looked up from the kitchen table.

"Boys, something very important is happening right now, something that we have been waiting for a long time. We cannot turn away from what people are doing down in Alabama. Remember we read about what was going on down there? Well, they are not riding the buses, right? I think that we need to support them, so I am sending them some money. I'm sending it to that church where they are organizing that boycott and, boys, nothing, not even your father, will stop me."

Mom licked the envelope and sealed it.

"Your father thinks it's a waste of our money, but I disagree. I believe with all my heart that we have to help one another, and this is the time to do it."

Marty and I stood and watched our mother; she had a look of determination that was new to us. We were convinced that what she was doing was the best thing anyone could possibly do.

Marty was the first to speak. "Mom, are you sending them money even though Dad said not to?"

Mom smiled at her own answer when she said. "I sure am." With that, she got up from the table and said, "Boys, find your brother and sister. We're all going to the post office, and we're going right now!"

That afternoon, my brothers and my sister and I walked to the post office on 63rd and Cottage Grove to send a check to help fight the hatred that thrived in our country, Mom led the way.

When Dad came home late that evening, we didn't speak to him. I was angry, not only because he yelled at Mom, but also because he wouldn't help.

Mom later explained that Dad had fought many battles in his life and like a lot of Negroes, felt that things would never change. Many believed that it was useless to "bang your head against a brick wall." But Mom and, fortunately, many people believed that change had to come.

The check that my mother sent was cashed by The Dexter Avenue Baptist Church.

With the help and support of people all over America, both black and white, the segregation of the bus system came to an end. On November 17, 1956, every citizen could ride on a Montgomery, Alabama, bus, seated anywhere they wanted. The South as well as the North saw many boycotts and sit-ins for years to come. The peaceful and successful response to unjust laws and unjust behavior began the change that America had to face.

It wasn't long after my mother's own protest against my father when our lives changed dramatically. It started when Dad came home one day.

"We got it!" Dad burst through the front door, clearly excited. It was early April 1957. Marty and I were playing Scrabble in the dining room that Saturday afternoon.

"We got it! Helen, we got it!" He was grinning broadly. I hadn't seen him this happy since I didn't know when, maybe never.

"We got it?" Mom was in the kitchen and had come quickly into the dining room, where she met my dad. They stopped and stared at each other. He reached out and held her hand.

"We got what?" Marty asked, his eyes still fixed on the letters he had drawn from the Scrabble bag.

"A house, Marty, we got it."

"Helen. We got it!" Dad's grin was immense. He had claimed his freedom, the freedom that had eluded him most of his life. He found it hidden in Chatham, a middle class section on the Southside of Chicago. The bid they had placed on the single-family brick home, with three bedrooms, back yard, and two-car garage had been accepted. We would be moving.

The spacious house they found was perfect. It stood on a beautiful street, shaded by century-old elm trees. For my parents, my sister, my brothers, and me, to have our own bedrooms meant we would have privacy and space. The house also had a huge backyard where we could play. Separate bedrooms, a basement, and a huge kitchen were an unfamiliar yet welcome luxury. My parents had achieved the American dream; they had found a safe, comfortable, and quiet place to raise a family.

We all took the news with mixed emotions. We had driven by the house that Mom and Dad wanted. It was in a neighborhood that was only three miles from our home. Those three miles were an extraordinary distance. It stretched from the comfortable enclave of friends and family that I loved to a community that was different, that I feared, because I felt it was dangerous. My brothers and I, unbeknownst to our parents, had ridden our bikes into that community the summer before.

It was in late July when I had been given a bicycle for my birthday. My brothers, cousins, and I decided to go for a bike ride.

"Man, Artie that is a cool bike." Jeffrey was impressed.

"Thanks. Look. It's got hand breaks and three gears. It's an English racer."

"Cool. Hey, fellas, let's go ridin.'"

"Yea, cool." Pete liked the idea, as did Marty and Billy. "Yep, us, too."

We took off on our bikes, down Vernon, across 65th, and then Marquette Blvd. We continued down Vernon Ave. We crossed street after street—71st, 72nd—when we started noticing there were fewer and fewer apartment buildings and more and more individual homes. When we crossed 79th Street, we realized there were no black people on the street in this neighborhood at all.

Our laughter and conversation slowly ended as we quietly pedaled down the street. We got to 80th Street, then 81st. The people we saw stopped what they were doing and watched us; some pointed. I'm unsure of why we didn't turn around, but we didn't, until we reached 83rd. We slowed down as we got closer to 83rd Street because what was ahead of us, across 83rd Street, was an empty field. Vernon Ave. had come to an apparent dead end. Jeffrey held up his hand and we all stopped in the middle of the street on the corner of Vernon Ave. and 83rd.

"You think we should keep goin'?" Jeffrey asked all of us but looked at Pete.

"I don't know. It looks like everybody around here keeps staring at us. Maybe we'd better go home."

The words were barely out of Pete's mouth when we heard the loud screech of car tires coming to a frantic stop. We turned around as two red-faced men jumped out of the car that had stopped right behind us. They walked toward us screaming profanities, pointing and waving angrily. Much of the filth that came out of their mouths I couldn't understand. But one thing was perfectly clear—our presence was unwanted.

We frantically turned our bikes around scrambling to keep out of the men's reach. Pete and Jeffrey stayed behind us making certain that Billy, Marty and I were safe. We rode down Vernon Ave. with the echoes of hatred following us. One word I did know, and it rang brutally, contaminating the air.

"NIGGER! NIGGER! GO BACK WHERE YOU BELONG!"

This was a Vernon Ave. that I did not know.

In silence we pedaled home, our joy gone. We had been assaulted, and it hurt, and it frightened me.

That night my brothers and I found the courage to relive what had happened.

"Pete, why did those men get so mad?" Marty whispered. It was almost a whimper.

"I'm not sure Marty, I just don't understand how..." His voice trailed off, and the night was silent.

After a moment, Pete began explaining why some people hated so much.

"Marty, Mom said that some people are just ignorant, and because they're ignorant, the easiest thing for them to do is to be a bully. So if they can bully you, then you can't see how stupid and weak they really are. Like those men today. I bet they are really very stupid. And you know what? I bet they wouldn't do that to dad or Uncle Jimmy."

"Yea, I bet you're right." I truly believed what my brother was saying was true.

"I bet Carol could beat them up, too!" Marty understood, so we were able to laugh at those ignorant men, believing they could not harm us. My brothers and I slept together as we had all of our lives. It felt good and safe to be close to them, even if Marty did wet the bed.

The night before we were to move, I listened as my mother talked with Aunt Monie.

"It doesn't seem real. We've lived here 16 years. All three of our boys were born here. I remember how lavish and huge this apartment seemed when we found it. Now it is so small, we've outgrown it."

They didn't speak for a while, but I could hear my mom and her sister as they drank coffee and ate cookies my aunt had made.

"We all have outgrown it," Aunt Monie agreed. "I think me and the boys will be moving soon also. I'm just not sure, with Jimmy and me, him leaving…." Her voice trailed off. I could hear a chair scrape against the floor as one of them got up.

"I'm so sorry to be leaving you now. Is there anything I can do? You know that I would do anything for you." It was Mom.

"I know, Helen, I know…. We'll certainly miss having you here. I'll certainly miss the children. I think of them as my own."

Aunt Monie sniffed a moment. It was strange, I had never known her to cry. "I think Billy will miss your boys most of all. Maybe he can spend the summer with you?"

"Of course he can, any one of them at any time." Mom's voice was soft and comforting. She was moving to a new place and the sister she loved wasn't.

I cried myself to sleep that night, crying because we were leaving so much behind.

Finally, on that Saturday morning, after weeks of sorting, packing, and discarding broken things, we were ready to move. The movers arrived in their overalls. They were big, burly men who went quickly about their work, carrying down to the big moving van our furniture, our clothing, and our lives. Dad and my brothers and sister had gone down to the car with the few boxes my mother refused to allow the moving men to take and were packing up the car.

Waiting in the apartment for Mom, I watched as she swept an already spotless floor. She had been up all night cleaning, making certain that the new residents of our home would find it clean and inviting.

"Mom...you ready?" I watched her stop at the sound of my voice. She waited before answering.

"I hope so, honey, I sure hope so." She smiled at me. "Are you ready, baby? Are you ready?"

I didn't know if I was ready or not, but it was time to move. The rest of our family was waiting for us. So I really didn't have any choice but to respond.

"Yes, Mom, I guess I am." I stood watching as she mindlessly wiped away another spot that wasn't dirty with a rag she had taken from her pocket.

"I think I'm going to like our new house. Are you...going to like it?" I asked.

She hesitated, then slowly nodded "yes." Then said very softly, "OK, baby, I suppose I can't clean up any more messes around here."

She then whispered to the air. "Good bye, and thanks." She looked around a moment more, then together, we walked out of the apartment and went downstairs to the car where our family waited. A late spring storm had sprung up during the night, so Mom and I hurried to the car before it started raining again.

Dad was quiet, as were my brothers and sister when we reached the car. Carol sat next to Dad in the front seat; she squeezed closer to him to make room for Mom. My two brothers, who were in the back seat, moved over to let me in. But Dad didn't start the engine immediately; he took a moment to really look at us all, then smiled.

"Well, ready or not, here we come." He started the car and pulled away from the curb.

As we slowly drove down our street, I looked out of the back window of our car. We were really moving. That was when I realized this might be the last time I would see 6425 S. Vernon. I was saddened deeply by that thought.

I looked at our apartment building. It stood erectly against the late spring morning; the rain storm had subsided for a moment. Through the car's window I could see just a sliver of blue sky and sun that a moment before had been hidden by heavy gray clouds. Maybe the storm was over, maybe it wasn't; it was hard to tell. Dad quietly guided our car away from our home. I settled back, sinking into my seat for the ride to our new house. I looked out of the side window, trying to absorb the neighborhood. That was when I saw an old friend. It was Mr. Malarcher, working in his yard, even in the rain. He had all of his gardening tools scattered about; some were leaning against his fence, others lay on the ground. It was planting time. He stopped what he was doing and looked up as the car passed his home. He saw us and slowly rose to his feet, took off that old hat of his, and began waving at me, waving goodbye. I waved back to him. I knew I would miss him and the neighborhood.

At that moment it began raining. The storm hadn't ended. It was just getting started.

Afterword

Recently, an investigation into the brutal murder of Emmett Till was reopened. I now believe this investigation should not end in the determination that others were involved because certainly there were. There are enough guilty parties complicit in the brutal act to indict nearly the entire country. Certainly, all of us who lived in America at that time are guilty. American society— particularly in the South, but not limited to the South—if it didn't condone, turned its collective disregarding eye to the truth of the hatred and bestiality that ran rampant through this country. If another co-conspirator is found, my fear is that this case will be closed and forgotten as it has been for the last 50 years. That would be as tragic as the murder. If this country is to find peace for all its citizens, it must certainly face the truth of its past and the truth of its present. It would be painful for many to honestly face that truth. But, as my mother would have said, "You have to be willing to face the truth to find the truth."

Over time, I have come to understand that I have always had to go into the pain to find the healing, because that is where I found it. The healing was in the pain.

The justice we all seek for Emmett Till can only come after we confront and wrestle mightily with the pain of truth; then justice can come and then healing. I will continue to work for justice and pray for healing.

To learn more about David Malarcher and Emmett Till, I encourage you to type their names into any computer search engine; you will find much. I have attempted to share with you a small story that falls between the lines of their historic resumes.

Epilogue

We are all shaped by our experiences, good and bad. It is often during those shaping, forming, and sometimes harsh experiences when we discover we are at our best. That is not to say that those experiences are not often difficult, because anything that forms or shapes you often requires that we stretch our self-imposed limits, and that can certainly be difficult; difficult but vital.

I have attempted to share with you, the reader, moments in my life that have formed me as well as the society in which I lived.

The years have taught me that the journey we all travel is often stormy; it is during those storms when we discover we can be excellent. We as a people, as a race in America, were at our best in the middle of our storms. We were at our best during the height of our struggle; our journey for freedom, as a consequence, became our destination.

Unfortunately, we fooled ourselves into believing our struggle was over. It wasn't. Still far too many of our people suffer from the devastation of racism. This truth is often denied, because it is too painful, too difficult to accept. But confront it we must, regardless of how painful it might be. The journey must continue, because without it we are lost.

The years that have come and gone since this story ended have been mostly kind and, of course, occasionally stormy.

My mother died as sturdy and elegant a woman as she lived; it happened July 16, 1999, in Chicago. We were all there.

Dad died a little over a year later. He was lonely without her.

Carol lives in retirement on the Southside of Chicago. She retired from the police force, a surprise to none. She never found her prince charming but does have two children, four grandchildren, and two great-grandchildren.

Pete is a scientist and lives in retirement from the Los Alamos National Laboratory, where he was deputy director. Dr. Warren F. Miller Jr. We still call him Pete. He has two sons and spends his time playing golf and volunteers with Big Brothers, Big Sisters. He graduated from West Point in 1964 and was a Viet Nam war hero for saving the lives of two of the men in his company. While at West Point, he was harassed by classmates who dressed in KKK regalia. They thought it was funny. Pete didn't.

Marty still lives in the Chicago area, where he owns an insurance training company. He trains unemployed and displaced workers. He married Penny, a wonderful woman he met in college; she's a school teacher in Naperville IL. They have three children. During the late 60s, Marty belonged to the Black Panther Party.

Andrea, our sister, was born after we moved to our new home in Chatham and lives in Chicago with her husband William. She patiently endures the stories we tell about 64th Street.

Mickey suffered a stroke recently and struggles valiantly to maintain his strength. He lives in Chicago with his wife. I hear he's still trying to win at Red Barber.

Jeffrey died in 1980. He was my friend and I still miss him. It is his son who wrote the foreword to this book.

Billy is a counselor and lives wonderfully in Texas. He is the author of the book *Dysfunctional by design*. He had a tryout with the Philadelphia Phillies in the early 60s— as a player, not a commentator.

Aunt Monie died in 1977. She was always a kind and wonderful woman. The best cook in the family.

Aunt Chris, Uncle Herman's wife, died in 1982; I always loved her German accent.

Uncle Jimmy died in 1959 from a broken heart. The cartoon characters he drew were stolen by a syndicated artist; he was never able to recover.

Frances died recently, I think it was 2001. The last time I saw her was at my mother's funeral. We talked for a moment.

Mr. Malarcher died in 1982 in Chicago. I missed the funeral. I read about it too late to attend. Good bye, Mr. Malarcher. Thanks.

Mrs. Lee still lives somewhere. She lived in your neighborhood when you were growing up, too. Thank God for Mrs. Lee.

Mr. Hamilton's store closed when Mrs. Hamilton died. I think it was 1960, just about the time big supermarkets began to open.

Mom and Dad and my uncle sold the farm in Michigan right after Emmett's murder. My parents used their share of the sale to buy the house in Chatham.

Most of my relatives, including "Little" Helen, Uncle Herman, and the Jacksons still live in the Chicagoland area. We still get together and remember.

I live happily in Connecticut with my wife Sandy. We have four children, and as of this writing, four grandchildren. I retired from Aetna years ago, then joined ING. I recently retired from there as well. I spend most of my time enjoying my family, visiting Chicago, and reminiscing. I was ordained a deacon in the Catholic Church in 2004 and work with the office for Black Catholic ministries. We try to provide opportunities for the community. I preach the Good News; I believe that there is hope for all of us. I continue to work for justice for all of God's children.

It is now your time. Go out and continue the journey. Be at your best.

Bibliography

Gilliam, Thomas J. "The Montgomery Bus Boycott of 1955-56." In: David J. Garrow, ed, **The Walking City: The Montgomery Bus Boycott.** Brooklyn, NY: Carlson Publishing, 1989, pp. 191-301.

Morris, Aldon D. **The Origins of the Civil Rights Movement: Black Communities Organizing for Change**. New York: The Free Press, 1986.

Ogbar, Jeffrey O.G. **Black Power: Radical Politics and African American Identity.** Baltimore: Johns Hopkins University Press, 2004.

Peterson, Robert. **Only the Ball Was White.** New York: Gramercy Book's an imprint of Random House Value Publishing, Inc., 1999.

Photographs

CPSIA information can be obtained at www.ICGtesting.com
Printed in the USA
BVOW060930150312

285182BV00002B/6/A